Guide To SHIPWRECK DIVING

Southern California

by Darren Douglass

Pisces Books
A Division of Gulf Publishing Company
Houston, Texas

Acknowledgments

Without the helpful cooperation and unselfish sharing of these individuals, this book would not have been possible:

Steve Barsky, Pete Brumis of the Associated Divers, Al Bruton, Chief Maritime Historian James Delgado of the National Park Service, Jack Drake, Nate Goodwin of the San Diego Harbor Police, John Hardy, Roy Hauser and the staff and crew of Truth Aquatics, Roy Hinrichs, Steve Lawson, David Lee, Ron McPeak, archaeologist, Don Morris of the Channel Islands National Monument, Tom Phillipp, Jens Rubschlager, and Bill Wilson.

In addition, the following organizations gave me invaluable assistance:

Allan Knight Maritime Museum, California Department of Fish and Game, Imperial War Museum of London, San Pedro Division of Todd Shipyards Co., Santa Barbara Historical Society, San Francisco Maritime Museum, United States Navy, and the Ventura Historical Society.

And, of course, my many wreck diving students who assisted in research deserve special thanks.

Dedication

For Stacey—
partner, co-laborer, model, editor, wife, and friend.

Library of Congress Cataloging-in-Publication Data
Douglass, Darren.
   Guide to shipwreck diving. Southern California/Darren Douglass.
     p. cm.
   ISBN 1-55992-004-1
   1. Shipwrecks—California, Southern. 2. Submarine diving—California, Southern. I. Title.
G525.D63   1989
917.94′9—dc20   89-35981
                                             CIP

Printed in Hong Kong

Table of Contents

Preface

Only those familiar with the underwater experience can fully imagine the adventure and excitement of wreck diving. Expectation accompanies each slow inhalation as you descend an anchor line through the blue depths. The heart rate quickens appreciably as you strain to focus on a faint shadow just below.

Slowly, a darkened hulk looms into view. You release the line and descend gently to the wreck. The circumstances of the sunken ship are mysteries or tales long forgotten by most. Moving down hallways and past bulkheads you feel a growing sense of awe: even here one finds beauty as air bubbles collide with overhead obstructions of wood and iron, collecting in trapped deposits that resemble reservoirs of liquid mercury. You exit the wreck and are greeted by teeming schools of fish and other more solitary marine dwellers.

The temporal nature of a shipwreck adds an alluring characteristic to the underwater scene. A gradual metamorphosis occurs as the old vessel deteriorates, yet with this change comes striking renewal. Eventually, the once dead ship will take on the colorful appearance of a living reef. Iron plates give way to rose-like anemones, bright stone corals, and encrusting sponges. Becoming a life-sustaining oasis in a sandy desert, the wreck provides habitat for blacksmith, kelpbass, perch, and thousands of other sea creatures.

By the time you have the opportunity to personally "discover" the wrecks described in this book, the ships themselves may have changed dramatically. Yet with each change something new is revealed. Wreck diving is not just the thrill of adventure but also the discovery of history.

Explore carefully when visiting southern California's shipwrecks. Indulge yourself within the safe limits of your bottom time. And remember, no matter how many dives you have made on a particular wreck, close observation always reveals fresh details.

Darren Douglass
Pomona, California

"Those who go down to the sea in ships, and do business on great waters, they have seen the works of the Lord, and His wonders in the deep." —Psalm 107:23–24

1

The California Coast

From the earliest times, southern California has been a land of surprises. To the Spaniards who first explored her coast, "Alta California" was unpleasant duty. Her interior could become blazingly hot. Water was scarce. Indians were plentiful.

But unbeknownst to the early Spaniards, Southern California was a hidden wellspring of valuable resources. After a rough and tumble period of colonization, small townships appeared along the shore. Intent on evangelizing the native Indians, Catholic missions began to flourish and engaged in the trade of hides, tallow, and wine. As trade grew, so too did the sleepy seaside villages as they welcomed visiting ships of commerce. Customs houses were established where taxes were levied for return to Spain. The most notable coastal hamlets were San Diego, San Pedro, and Santa Barbara. The land the early conquistadors had dryly dubbed "the hot furnace" had become a land flourishing with ranches, vineyards, and opportunity.

It was the lure of sea otter pelts that drew some of the earliest Yankee traders in the late 1700s. They were soon joined by British and Russians. When Mexico won its independence from Spain in 1822, California became a Mexican province. The United States defeated Mexico in 1848 and was given California as part of the peace agreement. Two weeks before the treaty was signed gold was discovered, and California was destined never to be the same again.

Gold fever, besides being the impetus for California's admittance to the Union in 1850, caused boom towns to spring up overnight. Maritime transportation to the golden shores became frantic. Scores of clippers and steamships soon plied the coastal waters and the famous "Panama Route" was implemented. Vessels from the eastern seaboard would land their travelers on the Panamanian isthmus, where they would embark on a dangerous and disease-ridden trail to the western coast. Here the miners, merchants, and missionaries boarded vessels bound for San Francisco. To get there, every ship had to navigate up the southern California coast.

The irregular contour of this jagged, rocky coastline, with its isolated islands and sheer pinnacles, presents hazards enough for most mariners. But California seas are also unpredictable. While sparkling in light, refreshing breezes one moment, the waters can quickly churn into ugly, mountainous seas lashed by a whip-cracking gale. Sudden fogs and squalls that roll down

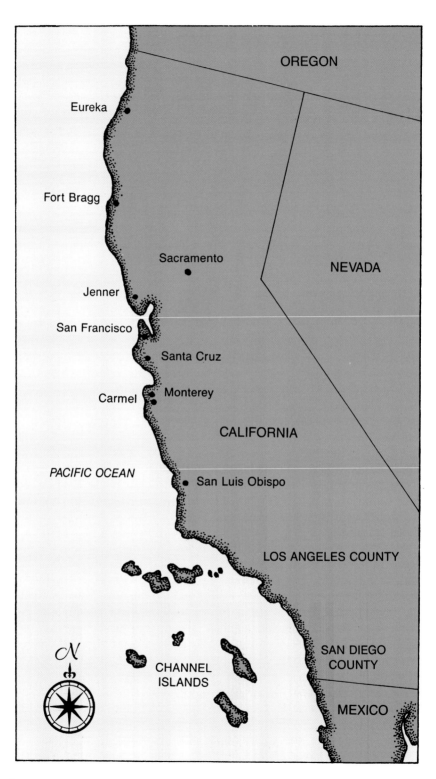

OREGON

Eureka

Fort Bragg

Sacramento

NEVADA

Jenner

San Francisco

Santa Cruz

Carmel   Monterey

CALIFORNIA

PACIFIC OCEAN

San Luis Obispo

LOS ANGELES COUNTY

𝒩

SAN DIEGO
COUNTY

CHANNEL
ISLANDS

MEXICO

from the north with seldom any warning add an even more sinister element to the dangers of collision with both kindred vessels and unforgiving shores.

From the days of the Spanish, when several of Manila's rich galleons were wrecked along the shore, to the present day, hundreds of ships and thousands of men never reached their intended destination. Many vessels sank alone—quietly and quickly forgotten. Others merited brief eulogies in newspapers. Presently, only a remembered few are being explored by divers.

Modern navigational aids have now slowed the attrition of vessels along the coast. But despite man's technological advances, the same violent conditions that bested mariners long ago continue to strike the 20th century seafarer, occasionally replenishing the availability of shipwrecks.

Currently, a new phenomenon—that of man—is at work sending derelict vessels to the bottom as artificial reefs. These planned sinkings at carefully selected sites not only present an ecological boon to the marine environment, but also add a valuable dive site where previously none existed.

Southern California wreck divers possess the best of both worlds; wrecks old and new in an environment rich in maritime and cultural history. While Spain's wrecked Manila Galleons and their cargoes of porcelain, spice, and silk continue to remain elusive, the conquistadors of long ago would be surprised to learn of the new "treasures" wreck divers are discovering and exploring beneath these coastal waters.

2

Local Conditions

Seasons. Good diving conditions are available throughout the year in Southern California. To be sure, there are certain times of year when more divers venture seaward than others. Yet each season has its unique features which have differing levels of appeal to individual divers.

Of course, surprises are always in store. Deserted beaches can be warm, sunny, and 80° in January. Conversely, crowded beaches can be cold and foggy in mid-August.

But when considering coastal diving conditions at various times of year, from Point Conception to San Diego, there are a few norms that you can expect with some accuracy.

Spring. Conditions from March to early May are the least desirable. Coastal canyon runoff due to rain and snowmelt can obliterate visibility off the beaches. Storms and squalls blow through the area with greater frequency, reducing visibility at the offshore islands as well. Increased levels of plankton can also affect water clarity.

The water temperature is at its coldest during this period, ranging from 52 to 56° Fahrenheit at the surface to as low as the high-40s at depth, making a quarter-inch wetsuit or dry suit necessary. It should be noted however that excellent diving days can occur in the spring, much to everyone's surprise.

Summer. The summer months are when the majority of divers hit the water. Visibility is usually good; approximately 15 to 25 feet off the beaches and 30 to 100 feet at the islands. Southerly swells generating large surf are common during this period and create strong surge conditions even at great depth. It is advisable to choose locations protected from the swell. Water temperature can rise to 75°.

Fall. Prevailing conditions are best in the fall months. Offshore breezes and the ensuing coastal upwelling provide the greatest water clarity. It is not uncommon to encounter visibility from 30 to 50 feet off the beaches, and from 80 to 150 feet at the islands. The water is still warm. Temperatures remain at about 68° at the surface and in the mid-60s at depth.

Winter. An extension of the fall season with just a slight drop in water temperature, winter is also a good time for diving. Violent winter storms, when they do arise, can destroy diving conditions. Yet the sea state will revert to normal a short time after the storm passes.

Plankton. One variable affecting visibility at any time of year is the presence of plankton. When plankton concentrations are high, visibility is usually destroyed. While difficult to predict, heavy periods of plankton occur only several times a year if weather and current patterns are normal.

Wreck Diving Equipment. In addition to standard items such as exposure suits and buoyancy compensators, there are several items necessary for divers to carry when exploring shipwrecks.

The first is an adequate air supply. Since many wrecks are found in deeper water, 80-cubic-foot cylinders are recommended. Divers planning to penetrate wrecks should utilize double cylinders or larger capacity cylinders. All wreck divers should incorporate the use of an octopus regulator or an A.I.R.II. Additionally, a redundant air supply such as an EBS (Emergency Breathing System) unit or a pony bottle is highly recommended. Divers with air driven tools should utilize twin cylinders with a separate manifold.

An essential item is a sharp dive knife because many of the wrecks are snagged with fishing nets, monofilament, and anchor lines.

Divers prepare to descend to the site of the Woodbury and Fuller.

A dive light will make a wreck diving experience more enjoyable by allowing the diver to inspect a wreck's darker corners and observe the natural colors of marine life.

Coveralls worn over the dive suit can be especially important in protecting wetsuits and dry suits when diving on older, iron-hulled wrecks. Sharp, jagged edges on these ships can in short order tear into an exposure suit. Standard mechanics' coveralls work well, but a lightweight cordura protective shell (used by offshore divers in the oil industry) is much stronger. These suits are now available to recreational divers and offer some distinct advantages. Cordura is not as heavy when wet, is machine washable, and is much more resistant to tearing and puncture. A good pair of heavy gloves are also necessary for protection.

Divers carrying a hardware store of tools (liftbags, marker buoys, chisels, pick hammers, lights, lines, etc.) can benefit by carrying these items on a full body harness. The harness allows for even distribution of the tools and their weight. It also allows divers to find the items more readily. Another option is to carry all tools in a tool bag designed for underwater use. Trained divers engaging in wreck penetration should also incorporate a safety reel.

Dive Techniques. Buoyancy control, natural navigation, and dive planning are all necessary skills for successful wreck diving.

The diver should be neutrally buoyant after descending the anchor line, otherwise he could go crashing to the bottom, which is invariably deeper than planned for. Crashing headlong into the wreck is guaranteed to stir up clouds of silt and reduce visibility drastically. By maintaining proper buoyancy, the visibility on a shipwreck will not deteriorate. An experienced wreck diver will assume a slight head down, fins up posture when swimming over a wreck site. This way silt is not stirred up by the fins.

Since some of the best wrecks are located in deep water, the diver must be skilled in natural navigation techniques. Once over the site, the dive boat's anchor line is the diver's ticket to the wreck and back to the surface. A diver must be able to relocate the anchor line at the conclusion of the dive. Making a free ascent from 100 feet in blue water can be exciting, but it can be dangerous as well. Ten and twenty foot mid-water safety stops are difficult to make when a diver is bobbing up and down in the swell. Loss of the ascent line can also mean drifting toward Japan if a strong current is running. The first thing a diver should do when reaching the bottom (especially on an unfamiliar wreck) is to study the area carefully. Draw a mental picture of port/starboard, bow/stern and any other structures of note that will serve as orientation points. Divers should choose an exploratory route with enough landmarks so they can return to the anchor line.

Good dive planning, of course, is of no value if the plan is not executed once underwater. It is critical not to exceed predetermined depth, bottom time, and minimum air limitations. Once on the wreck site air consumption should be monitored frequently. It does a diver little good to know where the anchor line is if there is not enough air remaining to get to it. Divers who are new to wreck diving will probably use their air faster. It is easy for divers to get caught up in the excitement of wreck diving and forget to pay close attention to their air supply. Monitor your pressure gauge closely.

Careful use of the no-decompression tables is of paramount importance. Work out your deepest depth and bottom time BEFORE jumping in the water. On a slate, jot this information down and carry it during the dive. Contingency plans for next greatest time and depth should be noted as well.

Penetration. Perhaps the most important area for wreck divers to consider is penetration. If you are not adequately trained or experienced in this element of wreck diving, you should not participate in such a venture.

There are two types of penetration. Full shipwreck penetration means there will be a complete loss of available light combined with overhead obstruction that precludes immediate ascent. As in ice and cave diving, penetrating a shipwreck requires specialized equipment and training. Primary and backup lights are needed. If penetration is deep and the exit route obscured, safety lines are necessary. In deep penetrations potential entanglement, loss of air supply, and lack of visibility mean mistakes and errors in judgment can exact a substantially higher price. Venturing deep inside a shipwreck has unique rewards of its own, but should be reserved for the experienced and trained only.

Deep inside the John C. Butler's interior lurks an occasional lobster.

7

Limited penetration where available light is always present and the exit area always in sight requires less experience and equipment. Nevertheless, special training is required for all types of penetration.

Wreck Dive Training. Beginning wreck divers who are not penetrating wrecks should be certified to at least the advanced openwater level. This will provide the necessary training in natural navigation skills (as a compass is rendered useless on an iron wreck) and the experience to handle situations where visibility is obscured.

It is highly recommended that a diver receive subsequent training through a wreck diving course offered by one of the national certification agencies. These specialty programs familiarize the student with the appropriate equipment and diving techniques needed to safely enjoy wreck diving and penetration. During the diving part of the course students will have the opportunity to gain experience in exploring local shipwrecks under the supervision of their instructors. As divers receive more specialized training and expand their underwater experiences, the more successful their wreck diving adventures will be.

Dive ratings. Throughout this book, all shipwrecks are rated according to the skill level the diver should possess before exploring them. Some ships will have multiple ratings because of varying conditions on different parts of the wreck. The ratings are as follows:

Novice. Advanced open water certification with little or no wreck diving experience. Novice wreck divers should do no penetrations and limit their depths to 80 feet.

Intermediate. Advanced training to include a wreck diving specialty course combined with a moderate amount of wreck diving experience. Intermediate divers should only practice limited penetration and limit their depth to 100 feet.

Advanced. Advanced training and extensive wreck diving experience. Very experienced in all aspects of deep penetration at depths up to 130 feet.

Marine life. The sea creatures that make a shipwreck their home are one of the special rewards of wreck diving. Shipwrecks provide divers with the opportunity to observe, photograph, and enjoy large concentrations of diverse marine life. Shipwrecks are congregational spots for marine animals, providing oasis-like habitats on an otherwise barren seabed.

The reef building process begins almost as soon as a ship sinks to the bottom. Algae quickly form a surface layer of crust for other plants to grow on. Pelagic as well as territorial fish are quickly drawn to the wreck for shelter and hunting purposes. Bryozoans and compound tunicates slowly begin to creep over the wreck site, followed by sponges, barnacles, and solitary corals. Hydroids and plume worms begin to grow along the wreck with chitons, limpets, and other members of the mollusk family.

As the food chain is established, more finned fish appear. High concentrations of fish are a regular feature of Southern California's wrecks. Blacksmith and senorita are almost always in abundance. Other fish common to local wrecks are calico and sandbass, croaker, sheephead, varieties of perch, swell shark, horn shark, and large lingcod. Colorful china, gopher, and vermilion rockfish are found scattered among rusting hull plates and pipes, using their distinctive color patterns as effective camouflage. Above the wreck, divers will occasionally observe teeming silvery schools of Spanish mackerel. These fish will swim over the wreck in a variety of traffic patterns, curving and undulating like commuter vehicles at rush hour. The sand flats next to the wreck are frequented by more visitors. Here, divers will encounter halibut, bat rays, pacific electric rays, sole, sand-dwelling anemones and angel sharks.

On the deeper wrecks, iron-hulled ships provide anchoring places for large orange and black mantled scallops, mussels, and feeder-extended barnacles. Here, divers will encounter a profusion of brightly colored corynactis anemones. Thick blankets of these pink, lavender, and white

Starfish, anemones, nudibranchs, and stone corals drape the Aggi's beams and masts.

club-tipped anemones can literally cover sheets of iron plating, ribworks, and beams. Colorful gorgonian seafans cover rusting bulwarks in a kaleidoscope of orange, pink, purple, and red. Spanish shawl, hilton, rainbow, and other varieties of iridescent nudibranchs inch their way along dilapidated railings and bulwarks. Navanax and sea cucumbers creep along water-filled hallways and hatches. Usually, divers will encounter large populations of colorful starfish searching for food among the other invertebrates. At times, groups of lobster will migrate to the base of a wreck seeking temporary shelter.

Beach divers, long familiar with their local reefs, will find an afterburner of new adventures on shipwrecks only a few miles away from their old diving haunts.

3

Santa Barbara-Ventura County

The Destroyers of Squadron 11

On the morning of Saturday, September 8, 1923, the men and ships of Destroyer Squadron 11 passed San Francisco's Golden Gate and steamed southward down the California coast. The ships had just returned from extensive maneuvers near Puget Sound with the Pacific Battle Fleet and were heading home to San Diego.

These were Clemson Class Destroyers built during World War I. They were nicknamed "four-stackers" or "four-pipers" due to the 4 tall smokestacks located amidships. Powered by 27,000 horsepower turbine engines, the ships could reach a maximum speed of 32 knots and maintain a cruising speed of 20 knots. These 314-foot-long greyhounds of the sea were considered to be the best in the U.S. Navy at the time and were packed with state-of-the-art machinery, communications, and fire control equipment. Weaponry consisted of a complement of four 4-inch guns, one or two 3-inch guns, and from four to twelve torpedoes. Consequently, there was little room left aboard these "tin cans," as they were also called, for crew comfort.

As Squadron 11 steamed southward under the overall command of Captain Edward H. Watson, his flagship, the Delphy, led the way. Behind the Delphy followed the destroyers S.P. Lee, Young, Woodbury, Nicholas, Fuller, Percival, Somers, Chauncey, Kennedy, Paul Hamilton, Stoddert, and Thompson. All were steaming in formation as they began what was to be a 24-hour test of their 20-knot cruising speed.

Shortly before noon the ships passed Pidgeon Point, their last visual reference. The fog thickened, forcing the four-stackers into a straight "follow the leader" formation, with intervals of 150 yards between ships.

The ships maintained their course and 20-knot speed into the night. Though each ship had its own navigator, the chief navigator aboard the Delphy was responsible for issuing navigation orders for the entire squadron.

In the wheelhouse of the Delphy, Captain Watson and Lieutenant Commander Donald Hunter had no landmarks or stars to help them navigate. Basing their position on an estimation of compass course and speed, the senior officers concluded that they had just passed Point Conception and were ready to make an eastward turn into the Santa Barbara Channel.

The squadron had one other navigational aid—the Naval Radio Compass Station at Point Arguello, 15 miles north of Point Conception. The Delphy, however, was the only ship authorized to signal the station, though the others could monitor transmissions. Just as the commanders were plotting their position as being outside the channel, the radio station signaled that the destroyers' course put them well north of the channel's entrance.

At the time, radio compass stations were relatively new navigational aids and many veteran mariners did not trust them. The stations operated by sending vessels two bearings—one from the station to the vessel and one, the reciprocal, from the vessel to the station. The signal "You bear 320 degrees true from us" was received on the bridge of the Delphy. The signal was assumed to be a reciprocal bearing which would have confirmed the Delphy's own estimated position. To avoid running ashore at San Miguel Island, Captain Watson ordered the squadron's course changed to 095 degrees.

In fact the squadron had unwittingly turned into an area north of Point Arguello with a longstanding reputation as the provider of fatal blows for many ships that sailed mistakenly near its rocky shores. Known as Honda, this graveyard of the central coast with its razor-sharp reefs, submerged pinnacles, fog, and heavy seas has claimed more than 42 vessels since 1815.

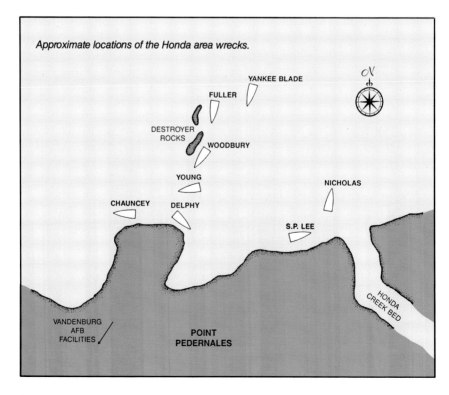

Approximate locations of the Honda area wrecks.

Squadron 11 ran aground at Point Arguello on the foggy night of September 8, 1923. Photograph courtesy of the Santa Barbara Historical Society.

Only seven minutes after Captain Watson ordered the change of course, the Delphy crashed hard aground in a screech of grinding metal and popping rivets. One by one, 7 of the 11 destroyers followed to their death.

Overview of the Wrecks of Squadron 11

Depth to top:	10'	**Built:**	1918–1920
Depth to bottom:	60'	**Sunk:**	1923
Average visibility:	10'	**Cause:**	Grounding
Expertise:	Advanced	**Type:**	Clemson destroyers
Current/surge:	Can be severe	**Length/Beam:**	314'/31'
Bottom:	Rock, sand	**Tonnage:**	1215
Location:	Honda/ Pt. Pedernales	**Condition:**	Scattered

1. Squadron 11 Flagship—U.S.S. Delphy

History: Commissioned in 1918, the Delphy (DD-261) was the oldest destroyer of Squadron 11. She was also the only destroyer in the squadron built by Bethlehem Shipbuilding in Squantum, Massachusetts. Her sisters were all built in Bethlehem's San Francisco yard. Before joining Destroyer Squadrons, Atlantic Fleet, the Delphy rescued survivors from the stranded ship Northern Pacific, off Fire Island, New York on New Year's Day, 1919. The Delphy later sailed to the west coast joining Destroyer Squadrons, Pacific Fleet where she conducted torpedo experiments off San Diego. On June 25th, 1923, the Delphy sailed north for summer maneuvers with the Battle Fleet in Washington. On September 8 of the same year, she was cruising south to home port in San Diego.

Sinking: As the lead ship in the column, the Delphy was the first to run aground. Less than 10 minutes after Captain Watson had given his order to turn the column eastward, his flagship's bow piled high onto the rocks. Immediately the Delphy sounded its crash siren to warn the ships astern that trouble was ahead. Heavy surf hammered her thin hullplates and turned her parallel to shore. Waiting for their chance between sets of waves, the men jumped ashore onto the oil-slick rocks. In short order, only the top of the Delphy's superstructure and her after turret were above water.

As the men began to abandon ship, a crew member jumped in the water, attempting to rescue several of his shipmates. His glasses shattered as he hit the water, causing splinters of glass to pierce his eyes. Blinded, he was pulled back aboard ship where he panicked and rushed wildly over the slippery deck, finally injuring himself further and becoming unconscious. The oil-soaked decks and pounding surf hampered the evacuation and the crew were unable to carry the injured man ashore. Orders were given to lash him to the mast until he could be removed without jeopardizing his rescuers. Shortly afterwards, however, the Delphy broke in half and sank. The man's body was found later, still tied to the mast. The final toll on the Delphy was three dead and fifteen injured. Only a small portion of the ship was ever salvaged.

2. U.S.S. S.P. Lee

History: The S.P. Lee (DD-310) was named after Rear Admiral Samuel Phillips Lee, who served in naval combat during the Mexican War and commanded several ships blockading confederate shipping during the Civil War.

Commissioned in 1918, the S.P.Lee spent most of her first two years in Reserve Destroyer Division with a reduced crew. Later she was rotated into active service and began conducting gunnery tests and torpedo exercises off the San Diego coast. In 1923 she cruised the coast of Washington with Destroyer Squadron 11 and put into Tacoma, Port Angeles, and Seattle as an escort to President Warren Harding's ship Henderson. On September 8, 1923, S.P. Lee sailed for home port in San Diego.

Sinking: Quick on the heels of the Delphy, the S.P. Lee had little time to react to the crash sirens and blinking lights. As she grounded near the Honda creek bed she was forced broadside to the shore. Sharp rocks ripped through her hull and projected into the number two fireroom, halting all attempts to unground her. The S.P. Lee quickly listed 35 degrees to port but the crew was able to climb onto the rocky shore without any serious injury or loss of life. Only a portion of her equipment was salvaged.

3. U.S.S. Young

History: The Destroyer Young (DD-312) was named after Revolutionary War Captain John Young. When commissioned in 1919 she entered the rotating reserve and spent her first two years in relative idleness. In early 1923 the Young participated in fleet exercises off Panama and later joined Destroyer Squadron 11 in drills off the Washington coast. The Young was later moored for a brief period in San Francisco and sailed for home port San Diego on September 8.

Sinking: The Young dutifully trailed the wakes of the Delphy and S.P. Lee. Once aground, the Young was quickly turned on her side by the propeller blades of the Delphy. Many sailors were hurled into the surf while others were trapped below decks.

Lieutenant Commander William L. Calhoun ordered his men to make for the port side and stick with the ship. Many men were able to climb onto the ship's keel, where they shivered in the cold fog and received constant soakings from the pounding sea. Strong surges of water washed over the ship, threatening to carry the men away. In panic, several men jumped into the swirling waters in an attempt to reach shore, but were carried away by the current and lost.

Chief Boatswain's Mate Arthur Peterson tied a line around his waist and dove into the tumultuous seas in an attempt to reach the wrecked Chauncey, which was nearby and in a less precarious state. He was finally pulled aboard the Chauncey, vomiting from ingested saltwater and oil. The line was made fast and 70 of the Young's crew in life rafts pulled their way hand over hand to the comparative safety of the Chauncey.

Twenty men from the Young were killed—more than on any other ship in the squadron. The number of injured men is unconfirmed.

4. U.S.S. Woodbury

History: Like many other destroyers built in 1919, the U.S.S. Woodbury (DD-309) slid down the ways at Bethlehem Shipbuilding's Union Iron Works in San Francisco only to find herself on inactive status in the rotating reserve. The Woodbury was named for Levi Woodbury, a New Hampshire attorney and judge who became Governor in 1822. Governor Woodbury became a United States senator in 1825 and went on to serve as Secretary of the Navy under President Andrew Jackson. An active national politician, Woodbury's final post was with the United States Supreme Court, until his death in 1851. Placed on active status in 1921, the Woodbury conducted 30-knot speed runs off the California coast and performed torpedo practice. The Woodbury later served as a "target" for long range gunnery drills, recovering practice torpedoes for the battleships Idaho and New Mexico. While touring the waters of the Pacific northwest, the Woodbury had the distinction of shuttling the Commander in Chief, United States Fleet, Admiral Robert E. Coontz and a party of congressmen to Coontz's flagship, the armored cruiser Seattle.

A diver exploring the wreckage encountered within the graveyard of Squadron 11.

16

The Woodbury later sailed south to San Francisco, conducting tactical maneuvers and exercises with battleships en route. After remaining in San Francisco for a week, the Woodbury steamed south with the destroyers of Squadron 11 for home port in San Diego.

Sinking: Following its errant flagship, the Woodbury executed the fateful turn to course 095 shortly after 9pm. Soon the Woodbury found herself wedged into a crevice between two large pinnacles that broke the surface. Heavy seas tumbled her from side to side, quickly ripping the destroyer apart at the seams. As water poured into the forward boiler and engine room compartments, Commander Louis P. Davis ordered full speed astern. Engineering officer Ensign Horatio Ridout and his men worked valiantly to produce the horsepower necessary to pull the ship out, but massive flooding snuffed out the boiler room fires.

Meanwhile, volunteers made fast a line from the bow to the rocky islet that would later bear the Woodbury's name. Heavy seas caused the destroyer to settle astern, while the constant bucking of the swell brought the bow up and down. Climbing the lines hand over hand, the crew was pitched back and forth on the way to safety as the line tensed and slackened. They were later rescued by the purse seiner Buena Amor de Roma. The entire crew escaped; only minor injuries were reported.

The last entry in the Woodbury's log aptly reflected the ship's status: "Woodbury on the rocks off Point Arguello, Ca., abandoned by all hands and under supervision of a salvage party composed of men from various 11th squadron ships." The Woodbury was salvaged twice but each attempt was only partially successful.

5. U.S.S. Nicholas

History: The Nicholas (DD-311), was named after Samuel Nicholas, who received the earliest recorded commission as Captain of the Marines from the Continental Congress in 1775. Captain Nicholas commanded the first amphibious landing of American Marines during the attack on New Providence, Bahamas.

The first years of the Nicholas were uneventful as she joined the rotating reserve after being launched at Bethlehem Shipbuilding in San Francisco in 1919. In 1923 the Nicholas found herself back at her birthplace after completing fleet maneuvers off the Washington coast. She set sail with the destroyers of Squadron 11 on the morning of September 8, 1923, bound for San Diego.

Sinking: Shortly after executing the change in course to 095, Lieutenant Commander Herbert Roesch quickly realized his ship was in trouble.

Hearing crash sirens and seeing the other destroyers tossed about on Honda's rocks, the men aboard the Nicholas frantically attempted to turn their ship back out to sea. Through a tremendous display of helmsmanship, the destroyer ran a desperate inshore circle through pounding surf. The gambit almost paid off, but inevitably the jagged rocks tore through her hull as she ploughed toward open ocean.

Hard aground on a submerged reef with her bow facing seaward, the Nicholas took a distinct list to the starboard. The crew remained aboard ship until daylight when a line was run to shore. There were no serious injuries aboard the Nicholas.

6. U.S.S. Fuller

History: The U.S.S. Fuller (DD-297) was named after Edward Canfield Fuller, a Marine captain who was posthumously awarded the Distinguished Service Cross for heroism in the Battle of Belleau Wood during World War I.

Built in 1918 at the Union Iron Works yard in San Francisco, the Fuller was not commissioned until 1920. She pulled a brief tour of duty cruising to the Hawaiian Islands, and later trained with the Pacific Battle Fleet off Panama and San Diego. In 1923 she conducted maneuvers off the Washington coast with Destroyer Squadron 11. On September 8 of that year, she began her fateful journey toward her home port of San Diego.

The Fuller. Courtesy of the National Archives.

Sinking: The Fuller struck the outside edge of an offshore pinnacle and began to list slightly to starboard. She settled until her main starboard deck was even with the waterline. As the sea smashed against her port side, the shivering crew climbed higher until they were huddling against the smokestacks for warmth.

Occasionally large waves would sweep the deck, carrying men over the side. Volunteers attempted to row a line to the nearby Woodbury, which appeared more stable than their own ship. Although they rowed all night, darkness and confused seas prevented the men from finding the Woodbury. The men had no idea where they were, but in the darkness they could hear screams from men aboard other grounded ships. Periodic flares were sent up and the men rowed toward them. They were, however, unable to reach their destination before the flare faded into blackness. Finally, dawn arrived and the volunteers reached the Woodbury and secured the line. The Fuller's crew joined the Woodbury's on the small rocky islet which became their sanctuary. A short time later both crews were rescued by Captain Giacomo Nocenti's purse seiner, Buena Amor de Roma. None of the Fuller's crewmen suffered more than minor injuries.

7. U.S.S. Chauncey

History: The U.S.S. Chauncey was named after Isaac Chauncey who, as a U.S. Navy Lieutenant fought with distinction in the West Indies and Mediterranean between 1779 and 1820. During the War of 1812 he

The Chauncey (foreground), Woodbury, and Fuller on the offshore rocks that spelled doom for the destroyers of Squadron 11. Courtesy of the National Archives.

Brass artifacts recovered from the Honda destroyers.

commanded the Naval forces on Lake Ontario and coordinated amphibious assaults with the Army. He later attained the rank of Commodore and went on to serve as president of the Board of Navy Commissioners.

Shortly after her commissioning at the Union Iron Works in San Francisco the Chauncey (DD-296) sailed to Hawaii while taking part in Pacific Fleet maneuvers and gunnery exercises. She later spent an idle year and a half in reserve. After returning to active duty, she became the flagship for Destroyer Division 31. With the other destroyers in her squadron, the Chauncey left San Francisco on September 8, 1923.

Sinking: Shortly after the Chauncey embarked on the newly assigned course of 095 degrees, the officers in her chilly wheelhouse heard the wail of crash sirens cutting through the night air. Rushing onto the bridge, Lieutenant Commander R.H. Booth looked off his bow and saw the blinking running lights of the Delphy, Young, and S.P. Lee at a dead stop and listing at extreme angles.

Commander Booth ordered hard left rudder and the Chauncey lurched her way through the battering surf. Slowly turning, she plunged through a cresting wave and slammed headlong onto a razor sharp reef. The collision knocked Booth off his feet and slammed him against the bridge bulkhead. The ship's wheel spun wildly and threw the helmsman to the floor. The Chauncey's crash sirens were soon added to the woeful chorus of suffering ships.

A short time after the Chauncey struck bottom, the Chief Boatswain's Mate from the Young swam to her side with a lifeline from his ship. The line was made fast and illuminated with lights. Slowly, survivors from the capsized Young made their way to safety.

The Chauncey was one of the least perilously grounded vessels and although she listed slightly to starboard, her midship decks were still two feet above the waterline. All her men made shore safely. The destroyer was eventually torn apart by the pounding surf.

Aftermath

In a single night during peacetime, the U.S. Navy lost more combat ships than in the entire course of World War I. The damages were estimated at $13,500,000. In human terms the casualties were 23 dead and 28 seriously injured. Most of the deaths were crewmen aboard the Young who tried to swim for shore.

A Naval Court of Inquiry was convened shortly after the disaster. The Court ordered the commanding officer of each ship as well as Captain Watson, Lieutenant Commander Hunter, and the Delphy's navigation officer to be tried by General Court Martial. They were charged with "culpable inefficiency in the performance of duty" and "through negligence suffering vessels of the Navy to be run upon the rocks."

The fault was finally found to lie with Squadron Commander Watson, Lieutenant Commander Hunter, and the flagship's navigation officer. Captain Watson was sentenced to lose 150 numbers on the seniority list for promotion and Lieutenant Commander Hunter lost 100 numbers. The navigator's sentence is not known.

Save for a few pieces of rusting metal on the shore, the only epitaph for the disaster at Honda is a salvaged anchor from the Chauncey which rests on a concrete slab atop a bluff overlooking the site.

Diving the wrecks of Squadron 11

The Site: The wreckage of the seven destroyers lies a short distance in front of Vandenburg Air Force Base. It is recommended that boaters contact

Colorful small Corynactis anemones and black-mantled scallops along the portions of the Woodbury and Fuller that lie in deeper water.

the Pacific Missile Range for permission before anchoring over the wrecks. On a placid day, Honda appears desolate and quiet except for the surge on the rocks and the wind whistling along the cliffs. Since public coastal access is restricted, this is a stretch of coastline that few Californians get to see, frequented only by fishermen and commercial urchin divers.

The Dive: A dive on the destroyers at Honda is an exercise in awe and humility. As one swims through this brass boneyard of ships, one cannot help but recall the sobering events of September 8, 1923. Beneath the surging waters the destroyers still remain, but the old hulks are a far cry from their former selves.

Lying at depths ranging from 10 to 60 feet, the destroyers are battered and twisted by countless storms and swells. Huge bronze propellers gleam in the sand, their glistening blades polished clean by the continual wave action and shifting sand. Heaps of anchor chain, boilers, valves, and huge pieces of machinery mark the final resting position of each ship. Shells, guns, and occasional portholes or hatch covers lie partially covered in the sand.

The debris of the shallower wrecks such as the Delphy, Chauncey, S.P. Lee, Nicholas, and Young is well scattered and strewn along the bottom. The Woodbury and Fuller are in deeper water and are consequently more intact. Although today the destroyers of Squadron 11 are no longer visible from the surface, divers can still bear witness to the magnitude of the tragedy.

Artifacts: Honda is often referred to as ''the brass capital of California'' due to the tremendous amount of marine scrap still littered across the bottom.

One of the reasons why the Honda area has been called the "brass capital" of California.

Since pioneering divers first began visiting the site long ago, the destroyers of Honda have yielded a tremendous number of artifacts. The list of recovered items is extensive and includes huge brass valves, portholes, hatch covers, fire hose nozzles, armament, swords, and old coins. In 1986, a diver recovered Captain Watson's Annapolis school ring and returned it to the officer's widow.

Hazards: It is important to note that Honda is not one of the West Coast's "garden areas" for scuba diving. Rough weather is the norm, along with low visibility and strong currents. Honda is definitely a dive for advanced and experienced divers, and even for them the diving "window" does not stay open long. These waters can quickly become treacherous, as weather is in a constant state of change. The waters can be calm in the morning, but approach gale conditions in the afternoon. Boat handlers visiting the area should be experienced, and should exercise extreme caution.

Photo Tips: Due to the low visibility caused by suspended sediment, Honda is not usually a photogenic site. The wrecks in deeper water such as the Fuller and Woodbury fare slightly better and offer a small degree of improved clarity. When the ambient light level is high, many of the shallow wreck sites can be photographed with available light, thus eliminating some of the problems caused by backscatter. For the photographer willing to take the time and effort to work around these conditions, the immensity of the wreckage provides awesome subject material. Be sure not to miss the heaps of anchor chain and the massive bronze propellers glistening off the silty bottom.

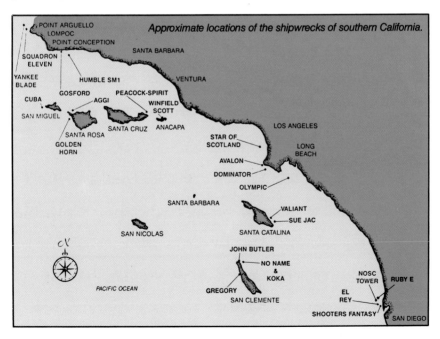

Approximate locations of the shipwrecks of southern California.

Drawing of the Yankee Blade.

8. Yankee Blade

Depth to top:	50'	**Built:**	1853
Depth to bottom:	60'	**Sunk:**	1854
Average visibility:	10'	**Cause:**	Struck submerged pinnacle
Expertise:	Advanced	**Type:**	Side-wheel passenger steamer
Current/surge:	Can be severe	**Length/Beam:**	274'/34'
Bottom:	Sand at base of reef	**Tonnage:**	1767 tons
Location:	Honda; base of boiler directly north of Destroyer Rock	**Condition:**	Destroyed; portions of machinery, sidewheel and engine remaining

History: After sliding down the ways at Perrine, Patterson & Stack's New York shipyard in 1853, the Yankee Blade quickly became one of the best known side-wheel steamships on the West Coast.

Drawing 21 feet of water, she was powered by dual side lever steam engines that drove the ship's massive paddle wheels. Each engine cylinder was 76 inches in diameter and had a twelve foot stroke. The steam boilers were 13 feet wide and 31 feet long. Designed to accommodate 1,000 passengers, she was owned by the Independent Steamship Company, operated by East Coast millionaire Cornelius Vanderbilt.

The Yankee Blade's presence on the West Coast was part of Vanderbilt's plan to wreak havoc on the Nicaraguan Steamship Line and compete with the Pacific Mail. Vanderbilt previously owned the Nicaraguan Line, but during a prolonged trip to Europe, his associates manipulated the company's stock and took control. Quickly reorganizing and forming a new company, Vanderbilt soon re-entered the west coast shipping business. Sending the Yankee Blade, North Star, and Uncle Sam to California was his way of retaliating.

The Independent Steamship Line struck back by offering cut-rate fares, and a price war ensued. Eventually, Vanderbilt struck a deal with his former associates to sell them his ships and stay out of the opposition steamship business. Under the new ownership of the Nicaraguan Line, the Yankee Blade's service on the West Coast was colorful, but short lived.

Sinking: On September 30, 1854, the one-year-old Blade was running out of San Francisco bound for Panama. The Blade's master, Captain Harry Randall, had made a bet with the captain of the Sonora that the Blade would reach port first. As the two vessels stood at the Golden Gate, a cannon fired and the race was on. Full steam ahead, the Yankee Blade plunged into a fogbank, charging southward.

The Blade carried an unspecified (estimates range from $100,000 to $2,000,000) amount of gold onboard. Reportedly, a local gang of San Francisco thugs known as "the Shoulder Strikers" had boarded the Blade intending to pirate the cargo. Unknown to the ship's officers, as the Blade churned down the coast she began to drift dangerously toward shore. Capt. Randall later speculated that the gang had crew members among their number who purposefully deviated the ship's compass to cause the Yankee Blade to eventually run aground.

Steaming at full speed the next day, the side-wheeler drove onto a reef less than a mile offshore near Point Arguello. The Blade was impaled amidships and, as surging breakers quickly broke her back, pandemonium spread among the frightened passengers.

Seeing their opportunity, the gang of thieves emerged from hiding and rushed for the purser's safe in the stern. They were thwarted, however, when the smashed aft quarter flooded and sank. The forward section of the ship continued to remain aground as the sea beat fiercely against it. At this point the frustrated pirates vented their hostilities by robbing and beating the panicked passengers.

Meanwhile, rioting crew members offered to ferry the highest-bidding passengers ashore. These boats swamped in the high seas, drowning all on board. Only those ferried ashore by Captain Randall reached safety. The remaining passengers were later rescued by the small coastal steamer Goliath. At the time, records were not kept on steerage passengers so the exact number of lives lost was never ascertained. Estimates of those who perished range from 15 to as high as several hundred.

The Dive: Today, the Blade's wreckage remains scattered along the top and base of the reef that sank it, in 15 to 60 feet of water. Many small pieces of copper and bronze lie embedded in the upper reef area mingled with a colorful array of central coast invertebrates such as local stone corals, anemones, nudibranchs and droids. There is often significant surge on top of the reef.

Larger, more identifiable portions of the ship, such as the massive remnants of the steam cylinders and broken portions of the paddle wheel, lie at 60 feet. One can also see connecting rods, brass fittings, and many unidentifiable iron machinery fragments at the base of the reef. Additional scattered debris is periodically covered and uncovered on the sand bottom as powerful Pacific storms move through the area. Most of the brass, bronze, and copper is polished to a bright sheen by the constant wave action.

Artifacts: Due to the large amount of gold reported to have gone down with the ship, the Yankee Blade has been the subject of intense salvage over the years. Soon after the steamer sank a gilt wooden eagle that once perched atop the Blade's pilot house came free and floated to the surface. The crew of a fishing boat found it floating near Point Arguello. The eagle is currently on display at the Santa Barbara Historical Society.

In November, 1854, the salvage vessel Dancing Feather reported recovering $68,000 worth of treasure from the wreck. Two chests containing

The rich waters north of Point Arguello allow colorful anemones to thrive even on the deeper-water sections of the Yankee Blade.

Gilt wooden eagle from the wreck of the Yankee Blade. Courtesy of the Santa Barbara Historical Society.

$34,000 were claimed to have been recovered by the schooner Pilgrim in January of 1855. The Blade's former master Harry Randall is said to have made the last major haul from the site, with divers bringing up more than $80,000 in treasure. Since then, two of the Blade's bronze signal cannons have been raised, along with fragments of the ship's bell, portholes, cage lamps, and a few gold nuggets.

Hazards: Due to the harsh weather that can roar down the central California coastline with little warning, boaters and divers should use extreme care when visiting the site. The same rock that broke the Yankee Blade's back more than 100 years ago still lies dangerously under the boiling surface.

Divers should also be wary of getting swept onto the shallows atop the reef when swells surge through the area.

Photo Tips: Visibility on the Yankee Blade, as true of many of the wrecks near Point Arguello, can be extremely limited. The larger pieces of wreckage near the huge steam engine cylinders offer the greatest degree of subject material when visibility is good enough for a wide-angle lens. The rockfish that congregate on the Blade's wreckage make good subjects as well. Even when sediment is not stirred up into suspension, divers should expect to find a greenish hue to the water. Good visibility on the Yankee Blade is considered to be 10–15 feet.

The Gosford. Photograph courtesy of the Allen Knight Maritime Museum.

9. Gosford

Depth to top:	20'	**Built:**	1891
Depth to bottom:	45'	**Sunk:**	1893
Average visibility:	10 to 15'	**Cause:**	Fire
Expertise:	Novice to intermediate	**Type:**	Barkentine
Current/surge:	Slight to severe	**Length/Beam:**	270'/30'
Bottom:	Sandstone with small rocks	**Tonnage:**	2251 tons
Location:	Kelpbed astride & inside Government's Point	**Condition:**	Relatively intact, but deteriorating

History: The four-masted barkentine Gosford was a British collier that used to sail from Europe to New York and take on drums of kerosene oil destined for the Orient. After discharging their cargo in the Pacific, the traders would then load ballast for the journey to the west coast. To make this leg of the voyage profitable, Australian coal would satisfy the needs of both ballast and commerce. Calling at Port in Tacoma, Portland, or San Francisco, the coal would be off-loaded. The final leg of the journey usually involved transporting a load of grain bound for South America or Europe. The entire odyssey could take a ship as long as two years.

Sinking: In November, 1893, the Gosford sailed northeast toward San Francisco carrying a load of Australian coal. While the ship was still hundreds of miles from land, a fire broke out below decks. Before long the flames spread to the cargo hold, ignited the coal, and turned the ship into a floating inferno.

While the officers and crew fought the conflagration bravely, the Captain realized that his ship was doomed. As conditions worsened he ordered the ship's boats loaded with food and supplies. The Gosford's sails were reset and the helm lashed into position so the ship would sail due east. As the Gosford sailed by itself, the crew boarded the long boats and attached themselves to the burning vessel by a rope. A hatchet-bearing seaman was on lookout at all times to cut the line if the Gosford suddenly took on water and began to sink.

For several days the crew of the Gosford trailed behind the blazing hulk until land was sighted near Point Conception. Nearing shore, the small boats cast off their lines and rowed to a beach slightly north of Santa Barbara. All hands escaped injury. The Gosford sailed into Coho Bay, just south of Government's Point, where she struck bottom and eventually sank. The ship and its cargo were both total losses.

The Dive: Teeming with an abundance of marine life, the Gosford is an excellent example of how the sea slowly turns a shipwreck into a living reef.

The Gosford is heavily covered by a dense kelp bed.

The Gosford offers a habitat for animals and plants that would not normally be able to survive in the area. Kelp coverage is extensive and the long, thin stripes wind their way toward the surface, creating a thick overhead canopy. Calico bass and kelp rockfish hide beneath the fronds.

One of the first things divers will note about the wreck is the thick carpet of anemones. The Gosford is the shallowest wreck in southern California to have such a colony of white, pink, orange, red, and lavender corynactis.

The Gosford's hull is still very much intact and it is possible to swim the entire length of the ship in a single dive. Some of the iron plates have fallen off the sides of the ship and formed miniature reefs of their own in the sand. Divers can swim through many of these structures. A short distance from the main hull, in a colorful jumble of iron, wood, and anemones, lies the Gosford's bowsprit. The fire-gutted hull is heavily filled in by thick layers of sediment and a labyrinth of colonial sand tube worms. Looking inside the holds where the Gosford carried its flammable cargo, divers will encounter loose chunks of coal, thick wooden planks of decking and occasional scraps of iron and brass. Several long pieces of the once elegant masts can be found inside the hull along with sheets of copper plating. Bare porthole openings can be seen along the sides of the vessel. The portholes, however, have long since disappeared.

Artifacts: The Gosford has been well known to the local commercial abalone and urchin divers for many years. While the prized portholes have been recovered over the decades, there could very well be more treasures waiting for those willing to fan the tremendous amount of silt in the hull or excavate to the lower decks.

Hazards: Surge in the shallow water near Government's Point can become strong during periods of large swells. The surge combined with the heavy growth of kelp winding to the surface increases the risk of entanglement, making a sharp knife an absolute necessity. Since the wreck is deteriorating, there are many sharp, jagged pieces of metal throughout the site.

Photo Tips: When visibility is greatly reduced, wide-angle photographers should consider using available light to avoid severe backscatter. While available light will provide clear images of the ship, the colorful growth on the wreck will not be apparent. Sitting upright off the sand bottom, the bow is the tallest and most dramatic structure remaining. Many of the iron support beams are still in place, covered with multi-colored, white-tipped anemones. The stern section has deteriorated more than other portions of the wreck but still allows for some interesting vertical angles. Here, several extremely large hull plates have fallen and now rest in the sand. Macrophotographers will enjoy the brilliant congregations of anemones, feather duster worms, sponges, and tunicates covering the entire wreck. Invertebrate life has been thriving on the Gosford for nearly 100 years, offering stunning subject material at every turn.

10. Humble SM-1

Depth to top:	60'	**Built:**	1945
Depth to bottom:	80'	**Sunk:**	1962
Average visibility:	20'	**Cause:**	Foundered in storm
Expertise:	Intermediate to advanced	**Type:**	Oil drilling ship
Current/surge:	Can be severe	**Length/Beam:**	180'
Bottom:	Silt and small rocks	**Tonnage:**	Unknown
Location:	South of Government's Point, Coho Bay	**Condition:**	Intact

History: The Humble SM-1 was built near the close of World War II as a U.S. Navy Medium Landing Ship (LSM-251). These amphibious transports were used to deploy troops, tanks, and other heavy equipment onto beaches. During the war 558 LSMs, including LSM-251, were built

The LSM 253 was the same class of landing ship as the Humble SM-1. Courtesy of the National Archives.

by Brown Shipbuilding of Houston, Texas. Originally LSM-251 was 204 feet long and driven by twin screw diesel engines. Most LSMs had two 40mm anti-aircraft guns on board; others were outfitted with rockets. Some LSMs were fitted with Kirsten cycloidal propellers, which enabled the ship to turn 360 degrees and remain in the same position.

LSM-251 was built too late in the war to see action. By the late 1950s, the Navy had scrapped, sold, or converted most of the LSMs in its fleet. The LSM-251 was sold to the Western Oil and Refining Co. In 1958 the craft was renamed the Humble SM-1 (Humble Oil, Standard Oil, and Mobil Oil Companies), and converted into an oil drilling barge at Todd Shipyards, San Pedro, California.

She was placed into service for Phillips Petroleum in the offshore oilfields between Ventura and Point Conception. In her new configuration the SM-1 was a combination of barge and ship. Engines removed, she was no longer able to sail under her own power and had a distinctive rounded hull design.

The SM-1 consisted of three decks and had powerful anchor winches at bow and stern. The vessel had an open drill well through the center which allowed the drilling shaft to descend directly to the ocean floor. The SM-1 carried a smaller crane on its main deck along with two 20-foot lifeboats. She also had on board a large complement of heavy industrial equipment including compressors, mud pumps, lengths of drill pipe, collars, and commercial diving gear.

Sinking: In 1962 Global Marine operated the SM-1 in a drilling project for Texaco south of Point Conception near Coho Bay. Twenty men were stationed aboard as the vessel sat in place at a six-point anchor. During the operation, a squall blew southward from Point Conception, creating heavy seas. While the men continued to work, the lurching groundswell caused the anchors to loosen and drag. The SM-1 was slowly being driven toward shore. In an effort to avoid foundering, the men sought to jettison the 1,900 feet of 10¾ inch pipe. Unfortunately, the diesel engine needed to operate the crane refused to start.

As the drill ship continued to drag its way toward the shallows, one anchor suddenly caught bottom, swinging the rolling barge into the swells, threatening to capsize the vessel. As the SM-1's troubles began, the oilfield crew boat, Helen, was standing close by to lend assistance if needed. Seeing the ship was doomed, several men leaped aboard the crew boat, one oilworker literally landing in the waiting arms of a deckhand. Like a breeching whale, the Humble SM-1 rolled onto its side and slowly descended beneath the waves. Remaining crewmen and workers leaped into the sea and swam for the crew boat. The Helen managed to recover all of the men, wet, but unharmed.

When the weather abated, divers began salvaging the valuable gear that remained aboard the SM-1. Underwater, the vessel still remained in a

Anemones cover the SM-1 like a vibrant tapestry.

precarious position because the drill well that drove into the shale sea floor suspended the hull 25 feet off the bottom. The stern quarter had settled to the reef and was now being ground into the shale as the ship pitched and yawed in the surge. A short time later the drill well finally snapped, settling the vessel on the bottom, upside down.

The Dive: Today the SM-1 is one of the most picturesque, intact, and easily penetrated wrecks in southern California. She still lies upside down in a sandy area interspersed with small, low-lying reefs. Kelp grows thickly on these reefs, surrounding the wreck. The hull is covered with vibrant and colorful marine life. Thousands of small, bright red and pink corynactis anemones carpet the ship's exterior like a finely woven tapestry. Orange and yellow Christmas tree worms extend their chrysanthemum-like plumes into the nutrient-rich current. Large white metridium anemones grow along the underside of the wreck like hundreds of hanging feather dusters. Blue, white, and yellow hermissenda nudibranchs creep along the algae-covered iron. Brightly iridescent, these dayglow gastropods resemble miniature neon billboards; the area looks like an underwater Times Square. Others, such as the hiltonhead and bright crimson rainbow nudibranch can be found contributing to the wreck's colorful decor. Kelp bass hover motionless over the site, casting a wary eye at the visiting diver. Inside the ship's darker crevices hide spidercrabs and olive rockfish.

Descending onto the wreck, divers should note the curvature of the SM-1's hull. The moon bay is situated in the center of the ship, looking like a marine architect's error. Here, divers can go through the hole and access portions of the main deck. The proximity of the seafloor beneath and the deck of the ship above means that divers have little room for turning around once inside. Another way divers can gain access inside the wreck is by venturing underneath the stern section. This is where the second anchor winch is located. Here, dozens of large white metridiums hang upside down from the deck. Lights are needed when venturing inside both of these areas.

There are also two openings that have been cut through the SM-1's bottom and starboard side, giving divers access to the heart of the vessel's interior. Divers can explore the entrances of these holes without a light, but farther inside, pitch darkness prevails. There are also passageways that branch off into other distant compartments. Several smaller openings have been cut into the port bow and also give access to the interior.

Artifacts: Many artifacts have come from the SM-1 over the years. Since the vessel is large and offers many avenues of penetration, there are still interior compartments that have not been thoroughly explored. Large brass pipes and valves, junction boxes, circuit panels and other items still remain attached to the SM-1. The large portholes have already been removed from the crew's mess and galley. Since the SM-1 was involved in the offshore oil industry, commercial divers were regularly employed on board. During the 1960s, heavy bronze Siebe-Gorman diving helmets were standard dress for the working diver. Several of these valuable helmets were stowed away

Porthole from the Humble SM-1.
Photograph by Steven M. Barsky.

in the diving locker when the SM-1 sank. According to salvors who first worked the wreck, they have been recovered. There are many silty debris pockets throughout the ship's interior. A careful inspection of these pockets could reveal many other items of marine memorabilia.

Hazards: The SM-1 lies two and a half miles offshore, open to the full brunt of the ocean. Strong swells can create a significant surge, even at 70 feet. Because of this, divers should be careful when examining the holes that give access to the ship's interior. Strong surge can stuff a diver inside, or pull a diver out. Since there are several sharp, jagged pieces of iron near these openings, the prudent diver will take care to avoid becoming accidentally impaled or slammed against a heavy iron bulkhead.

Powerful currents are often present at the wreck site. When this is the case, divers should take care to pull themselves down the anchor line onto the wreck to avoid becoming swept off the site. The current can also flatten the nearby kelp strands over the top of the wreck, covering much of it from view. Take care to look underneath the kelp if you think you have missed the wreck.

Photo Tips: This wreck is one of the most photogenic. There is enough invertebrate life on the SM-1 to keep a macrophotographer busy for many dives. For those photographers seeking wide-angle interior shots, there are also many opportunities. The hole cut in the SM-1's keel joins the opening in the starboard side via a large connecting compartment. Inside, much of the machinery, and many pumps and valves still remain. Photographers will find this to be an excellent spot for interior shots or for working with a model.

In short, the SM-1 is truly one of southern California's greatest wreck dives. Excellent subject material for all types of photographers is an extra bonus.

11. Cuba

Depth to top:	Boilers out of water at low tide	**Built:**	1897
Depth to bottom:	25'	**Sunk:**	1923
Average visibility:	30-40'	**Cause:**	Grounding
Expertise:	Advanced	**Type:**	Passenger/cargo steamer
Current/surge:	Heavy surge with swell action	**Length/Beam:**	307'/42'
Bottom:	Rocky reef	**Tonnage:**	3168
Location:	Point Bennett, San Miguel Island ("Foul Area")	**Condition:**	Scattered

History: The Pacific Mail Steamship Cuba, was originally built as the Coblenz in Hamburg, Germany in 1897. This large passenger and freight carrier was powered by a triple-expansion steam engine that turned a single propeller. During her time as a German vessel her name was changed to Sachem. Shortly after World War I she came under American ownership as a war prize. The U.S. Shipping board sold her to the famous Pacific Mail Steamship Line. The vessel was renamed Cuba and was assigned to the Panama-San Francisco route.

Sinking: On September 8, 1923 the Cuba plunged northward through heavy coastal fog, bound for San Francisco. Due to the persistently poor visibility, Captain Charles Holland had been unable to shoot the sun for the past three days. When evening came, the captain left orders to be called if visibility dropped below 5 miles. He also ordered soundings to be taken at midnight, and then retired to his cabin. Second Officer John Rochau was on the bridge during the midnight watch. He calculated the Cuba's position and estimated visibility to be four miles, yet he ignored the captain's standing orders to be called to the bridge. Hours later, First Officer Frank Wise stood watch and called the captain immediately.

Captain Holland came to the bridge and ordered an immediate change of course. Even before soundings could be taken, however, the Cuba struck a submerged pinnacle off Point Bennett, San Miguel Island. The 307-foot ship ground to a noisy halt.

In the lowest part of the ship, pandemonium broke out among the steerage passengers. As water poured inside their quarters, panic ensued, until a crew member took charge and evacuated them to the upper decks. Here the passengers saw that the Cuba was not in immediate danger of sinking. All passengers were then transferred to shore in the open boats.

The Cuba's predicament was made more difficult because the radio generator was out of commission and she could not call for help. The first officer, one passenger, and twelve crewmen rowed a lifeboat blindly in the fog until they sighted the Standard Oil tanker W.S. Miller. The Miller radioed word of the disaster back to the mainland.

Two nearby destroyers, the Reno and Selfridge, were steaming south of Point Conception making a speed run from San Francisco to San Diego. They were dispatched to the rescue. At daybreak they picked up the passengers, mail, liquor (national prohibition was still in effect) and 2.5 million dollars' worth of silver bullion. The Cuba remained above water for some time, undergoing extensive salvage. Finally the incessant waves pushed the Cuba off the rocks and it promptly sank.

The Dive: One of the special aspects of diving the Cuba is that large boats cannot safely approach the wreck site. When the Point Bennett foul area is approachable, however, smaller boats can slide in near the wash rocks on the northwest side, allowing divers access to the Cuba's final resting place.

The absence of the large commercial boats means divers will find the site pleasantly uncrowded.

Northernmost of the Channel Islands, San Miguel's remote Point Bennett juts far out into the open, unhindered Pacific. Fed by clear ocean currents, area water clarity is often exceptional, allowing visiting divers to view much of the Cuba from the surface.

Plates, beams, and boilers lie in the open on the rocky bottom. Twisted shards of iron, brass, and copper are scattered throughout the site, offering mute testimony to the ocean's destructive handiwork in transforming the former steamship into a montage of maritime debris.

Divers will encounter massive I-beams, lengths of mast, and rigging, all covered with a mantle of heavy marine growth. The glimmer of brass, copper, or bronze can occasionally be seen among the wreckage. While most decking has collapsed into the hull, divers can swim beneath fallen hull plates and broken bulwarks to view the porcelain toilets and sinks, and if lucky, one of the rare remaining portholes. Short strands of kelp rise from the bottom, lightly surging in the gentle ebb and flow. Large sheepshead, lingcod, and brightly iridescent red rockfish inhabit the wreck.

Artifacts: A local Santa Barbara resident, Ira Eaton, salvaged much of the Cuba shortly after it came to grief on the rocks. Due to a technicality of maritime law, Eaton and his cohorts legally were able to remove brass fittings, deckchairs, provisions, radio sets, doors, windows, galley utensils, linen, curtains, and some of the cargo of coffee.

Since the Cuba sank to the bottom of the reef, visiting divers have discovered her to be a fine producer of portholes and other marine artifacts. At present, however, the Cuba is protected by the National Park Service. San Miguel Island, like its neighboring islands to the south, is now part of the Channel Islands National Park. It is illegal to remove artifacts from any shipwreck within park boundaries.

Hazards: Due to the shallow depth of the wreck and the open ocean swells that crash onto San Miguel, the Cuba can have severe surge which is dangerous for both divers and boaters. Generally when it is calm enough to allow a boat to anchor, divers will encounter few difficulties.

Because of Point Bennett's large sea lion and elephant seal populations, great white sharks are known to frequent the area. Therefore, divers should plan on descending directly to the wreck and ascending directly to the boat. Long surface swims should be avoided. While divers have encountered white sharks on occasion, no serious injuries have ever been sustained in this area.

Photo Tips: A collapsing portion of the Cuba's bow presents some good angles for wide-angle shooting. The structure rises off the bottom about 15 feet, presenting some dramatic lines and symmetry. Two massive anchors rest nearby, flanked by piles of rusting chain.

Be on the lookout for large sea lions and elephant seals which often buzz through the area. These big creatures can surprise unwary wreck explorers, but provide exciting photo subjects—if you're quick enough.

12. Goldenhorn

Depth to top:	20'	**Built:**	1883
Depth to bottom:	30'	**Sunk:**	1892
Average visibility:	15' to 30'	**Cause:**	Ran aground in fog
Expertise:	Intermediate	**Type:**	Barkentine
Current/surge:	Strong surge in shallows	**Length/Beam:**	268'/40'
Bottom:	Rocks and boulders	**Tonnage:**	1915
Location:	Southwest shore of Santa Rosa Island (inside of Bee Rock)	**Condition:**	Broken up

History: The Goldenhorn and her sister ships Silberhorn and Matterhorn were built in 1883. They were designed by Glasgow shipbuilders Russell & Company for British merchant Charles E. de Wolf of Liverpool. These vessels were representative of the secondary transitional phase from clipper to big carrier. At the time, four-masted barques of iron and steel were a

The Goldenhorn. Courtesy of the San Francisco National Maritime Museum.

relatively new innovation. Predecessors of the larger-capacity barques of the late 90s, the Goldenhorn and her sisters were built for utility and function rather than for speed.

De Wolf's ships engaged in transcontinental trade from Britain to New South Wales and the West coast of the United States. The Goldenhorn busied itself in this route, as did the barque Gosford. The ship's journey began in its home port of Liverpool and completed the predictable circumnavigation of the world via the eastern seaboard of the United States, the Orient, and then Australia to pick up coal bound for the west coast. After discharging its sooty cargo in San Francisco or San Pedro, the ship would usually load grain or hides and set sail on the final leg of the journey. Once around Cape Horn, she would beat her way back to the British Isles where she would off-load and prepare for the next voyage.

Sinking: September 12, 1892, found the four-masted Goldenhorn sailing east with 1,800 tons of Australian coal destined for the mighty iron horses of the Southern Pacific Railroad. Enveloped in a thick fog, the Goldenhorn continued on, propelled by a light wind. Unwittingly, her bow was cutting a path directly towards Santa Rosa, one of the Channel Islands off Santa Barbara.

In the mist, a lookout's cry of "Land ho!" startled Captain Dunn and his crew of 28. Rapid efforts were made to change course, but as the ship sailed past Bee Rock, the wind slackened further. With her sails empty, the ship became unresponsive to the helm. Inevitably, the bow struck bottom and the surging waves smashed the Goldenhorn hard onto a submerged reef, dumping her anchors on impact.

The heavy swell rapidly tore the stern quarter apart as the crew put out in small boats. The crew found safety at Beecher's Bay but after finding that portion of the island uninhabited, they set out again for the open sea. Twenty-four hours later, having rowed for over 50 miles, they reached the mainland near Santa Barbara.

Word of the wreck rapidly spread along the Santa Barbara waterfront. Enterprising residents were quick to salvage what they could before the Goldenhorn finally succumbed to the waves and sank to the bottom of the reef.

The Dive: The wreckage from the Goldenhorn covers an extensive area in the shallows on the western side of Santa Rosa Island. The ship's structures are beaten down to reef level and flattened against the rocks. Still, much remains to be seen. Heavy steel plates lie broken, bent, and scattered across the rocky bottom. Large girders, mastworks, rigging, and an intact upper portion of the Goldenhorn's bow are spread over the reef like a pile of matchsticks. The huge capstan from the forward deck now rests atop a

This photo was taken during the National Park Service's mapping of the Goldenhorn site. Here, a diver examines one of the ship's mast steps. Note the ribwork in the background. Photograph by Steven M. Barsky/ Diving Systems International.

jumble of boulders. Heaps of anchor chain rest nearby. Bitts, and cleats remain fastened to deckplates.

Because of the shallow water, visibility can be limited and surge can range from a gentle back and forth motion to the ride of a tumultuous roller coaster. In fact, divers often explore the wreck while surging across the bottom. When an interesting item is encountered, a diver must hold onto a portion of the ship to remain in one place and inspect the object more closely.

Unlike many of the other Channel Island shipwrecks, invertebrate life on the Goldenhorn is relatively scarce, save for purple sea urchins and the occasional lobster and nudibranch. Fish, however, do thrive on the site. Schools of perch, senorita, and wrasse always seem to be present. Inside collapsed bulwarks and rusting crevices lurk cabezon and varieties of rockfish.

Channel Island National Park archaeologists have been actively sketching the wreckage to produce maps of the Goldenhorn's features. When completed, these maps will allow divers to identify various parts of the wreck and make sense of what might otherwise resemble a pile of jumbled debris.

Artifacts: Over the years many artifacts have been recovered from the Goldenhorn. These include several large and small portholes and steel letters bearing the ship's name and port of registry, Liverpool. Presently, as with all wrecks in the Channel Islands National Park, no artifacts may be lawfully taken.

Hazards: Due to the shallow depth and location on the exposed seaward side of Santa Rosa Island, the Goldenhorn is prone to surge conditions.

When surge is slight to moderate, a relaxed diver can visit with little difficulty. When surge is strong, however, diving is not recommended. Strong water movement and lowered visibility can easily cause a diver to ram into one of the sharp iron structures that protrude from the Goldenhorn. Boaters should also take care when moving close to shore, because a dragging anchor could spell disaster.

Photo Tips: Due to the limited visibility often encountered, photographers may achieve better results when utilizing available light. This helps avoid heavy backscatter that can be caused by strobe use. Divers should take special care of their 15mm lenses because of the surge.

13. Aggi

Depth to top:	20'	**Built:**	1894
Depth to bottom:	60'	**Sunk:**	1915
Average visibility:	30' to 60'	**Cause:**	Grounded in heavy weather
Expertise:	Intermediate to advanced	**Type:**	Barkentine
Current/surge:	Slight to severe	**Length/Beam:**	265'/35'
Bottom:	Rocky reef	**Tonnage:**	1751
Location:	Talcott Shoals, Santa Rosa Island	**Condition:**	Scattered atop a reef

History: Originally built in Glasgow as the Aspice, the 3-masted barkentine Aggi was registered in Lyngnor, Norway. She also served under the names Sant' Erasmo and Seerose. For 21 years she performed her duties as a grain carrier without mishap. Except for a few American, French, and German ships, the majority of the grain fleet were of British registry. The Aggi was one of the rare Norwegian vessels that competed for this cargo.

Sinking: On April 29, 1915, the Aggi departed San Francisco's Golden Gate in tow of the steamer Edgar R. Vance. Bound for Panama, the Aggi's hold carried 2,500 tons of barley and 600 tons of beans. Twenty men were aboard the vessel as she set out in an unusually cold gale. The temperatures were so frigid that the coastal mountains from San Francisco to Santa Barbara county hosted snow-capped peaks. The seas were high, built by a wind that whipped the railings with a cruel lash. Seventy-five miles south of San Francisco the weather deteriorated further, forcing the Vance to release the towing hawser and leaving the Aggi to sail on its own.

To make matters worse, the superstitious crew was concerned with a series of ominous signs. First, the ship's cat abandoned the vessel in port. Then the cabin boy died at the start of the voyage. The men noted that seabirds following the vessel screeched mournful cries as the Aggi surged her way down the coast. One gull, crewmembers claimed, perched on the mast at the start of the journey and did not cease its woeful crooning until disaster struck.

As the storm increased, the cargo in the Aggi's hold began to shift. Soon the freight had moved so far to leeward that the ship's rail cut beneath the surface and the crew's quarters filled with seawater. Damp and chilled, the men had to double bunk in the higher windward side of the ship.

On May 4 the Aggi neared the Channel Islands. Rather than continue to let the ship take a dangerous beating in open sea and risk capsizing, the captain, unaware of the dangerously shallow reefs of Talcott Shoals, began to traverse the passage between San Miguel and Santa Rosa Islands. The vessel struck bottom and quickly grounded. Attempts to free the iron-hulled ship were unsuccessful: the Aggi held fast.

All hands except the master and first mate, who stayed aboard to guard the cargo, took to an open boat and struck out for shore. The boat was intercepted by Santa Barbara resident, Captain Ira Eaton in the Sea Wolf who transferred the crew to shore. The officers followed shortly thereafter. As the hull of the Aggi was continually pounded by the seas, small leaks appeared, wetting the ship's cargo. Once wet, the grain expanded, causing the Aggi's steel plates to burst apart. Only a small portion of the cargo was saved. Broken and dying, the Aggi remained atop Talcott Shoals for some time before succumbing to the sea.

The Dive: Scattered debris from the Aggi lies a short distance from Santa Rosa Island in depths ranging from 20 to 60 feet. In the shallower waters divers will discover many beams and iron plates, now adorned with a rich blanket of urchins, anemones, and tube worms. A careful search will also reveal one of the Aggi's anchors, the shank of which is over 6 feet long.

A second anchor of the same size was salvaged by dive boat Captain Glen Miller and was donated to the Santa Barbara Historical Society where it is now on display in front of the society's museum.

In the same area as the anchor are the Aggi's capstan and large links of anchor chain. Descending the sloping reef, divers will encounter even larger iron plates, twisted and buckled from the pounding seas. Underneath these, spiny lobsters are often in residence. Along the slope are the long iron masts and boomworks, now home to horn sharks and cabezon.

The wreckage becomes more extensive in 60 feet of water. Besides additional iron plates and portions of masts, the Aggi's shattered aft section rises about 10 feet from a jumbled heap on the bottom.

The crumbled stern section of the Aggi; at 60' this is the deepest part of the wreckage.

One distinct advantage of a dive on the Aggi is that Talcott Shoals offers clear water and abundant marine life. Located on Santa Rosa Island's northern corner, which faces neighboring San Miguel Island, the Aggi is often prone to a moderate prevailing current which keeps the water blue and clear except during the spring months when plankton reduces visibility.

Colorful filter-feeding invertebrates such as anemones, tube worms, gorgonians, orange- and black-mantled scallops, and stone corals thrive in the current and present a dazzling array of subaquatic hues. Larger fish also frequent the area. Skirting along the deeper portions of the reef are gargantuan sheepshead and the occasional, but curious, black sea bass. Lingcod, cabezon and a large species of rockfish are often present. Schools of perch swim around the rusting beams and hollow masts. Because of the diversity of fish on the Aggi, it is noted as a productive site for bagging dinner. As a special treat, playful California sea lions sometimes surround divers with their underwater acrobatics.

The Aggi can be tough to locate at times because Talcott's reef system contains many short walls and ledges that can stymie a depth finder. Even with the help of Loran-C, most dive boats have a scouting diver descend to pinpoint the exact location. And, they are not always successful on the first attempt.

One of the Aggi's anchors on display
at the Santa Barbara Historical Society.

Artifacts: Prior to its inclusion in the Channel Islands National Park, the Aggi was a good producer of brass artifacts, including cage lamps and the occasional porthole. No artifacts may be removed from wrecks within park boundaries. Today the only "taking" on the Aggi, like other Channel Islands wrecks, is of photographs.

Hazards: Because of the prevailing current divers should work forward into the current from where their boat is anchored. Divers can then have the luxury of drifting back to the dive boat upon completion of the dive. The unwary could conceivably find themselves sailing down current towards neighboring Santa Cruz Island.

Photo Tips: The Aggi is extremely photogenic even though many of the structures have collapsed to the reef. The masts, overgrown with bright red and white spotted-rose anemones, stone corals, gorgonians and colorful tube worms, are a great place for wide-angle and extension-tube photography. Photographers seeking larger pieces of wreckage will find ample material in the stern section located at the bottom of the reef.

This minesweeper is believed to be of the same class as the Spirit of America/Peacock. Courtesy of the National Archives.

14. Peacock/Spirit of America

Depth to top:	45'	**Built:**	Early 1940s
Depth to bottom:	60'	**Sunk:**	Early 1970s
Average visibility:	30' to 40'	**Cause:**	Unknown
Expertise:	Novice to advanced	**Type:**	Minesweeper, possibly Falcon Class
Current/surge:	1 to 2 knot current usually prevails, minimal surge depending on swell direction	**Length/Beam:**	144'/27'
Bottom:	Sand	**Tonnage:**	950 tons
Location:	Scorpion's Anchorage, Santa Cruz Island	**Condition:**	Relatively intact, but deteriorating rapidly

History: This former U.S. Navy minesweeper is one of southern California's most enigmatic wrecks. To many divers, she is known as the Peacock, while to others she is the Spirit of America. The true story of her history is sketchy at best, surrounded by a cloud of conjecture, rumor, and waterfront yarns.

45

What is known is that the old minesweeper lay moored at Scorpion's Anchorage in a neglected state for at least three months during the early 1970s. Several Santa Barbara-based boat operators claim that the vessel also spent some time ashore at Scorpion's Anchorage where equipment, marine hardware, and timber was removed from the wooden-hulled ship.

Sinking: Reportedly the ship was towed off the beach to Scorpion's Anchorage where, in 60 feet of water, she slowly settled to the bottom. Divers hired by an insurance company reported that the minesweeper's seacocks had been intentionally opened.

The Dive: As the most intact wreck in the Channel Island chain, this minesweeper must be ranked as one of the premier dives on the coast. She sits upright with a slight port list, her bow pointing seaward. Divers descending to the wreck will usually encounter a large school of blacksmith circling the highest portion of the vessel. During the warm summer months, thousands of silvery Spanish mackerel join the scene, enveloping the wreck in an explosion of moving, mirrored light. Numerous spotted-rose anemones can be found among the deteriorating decks, and Spanish shawl nudibranchs creep throughout the rotting beams and timbers.

But the Santa Cruz minesweeper is a shipwreck in transition. With the passage of each year, further deterioration of the wreck is evident. Most of

A diver approaches the bow of the Spirit of America/Peacock.

the decking is gone and as the ship unfolds itself, access is opened up to more of the lower deck compartments. The entire wreck can be penetrated, allowing divers to swim from the rudder compartment to the chain locker without the necessity of a dive light. Rotting beams and hull planks allow sunlight to pierce most of the wreck's holds.

Divers can explore the brittle ribworks supporting the bow section. The chain hawser of the blunt-nosed bow rises 20 feet from the sand. The wheelhouse and superstructure have long since vanished but the crow's nest and antenna mast lie in the sand on the vessel's port side. Other wreckage near the mast provides refuge for sculpin and octopus.

A diver can swim the entire length of the wreck in a single dive because of the available bottom time. With its abundant marine life and dramatic structures, the minesweeper is one of the most picturesque and exciting wrecks along the coast.

Artifacts: The wreck lies within the Channel Islands National Park. Removal of artifacts is prohibited.

Hazards: While usually a well-protected site, during strong northwest swells and winds divers should avoid the anchorage.

Much of the wood on the wreck is in an extreme state of deterioration. Divers should be extremely cautious not to bump a wooden support that could collapse, bringing iron beams, deck cleats, and other large metal objects down on top of them.

Located in the forward lower deck is a large compartment with an iron hatch that still swings on its hinges. No sunlight penetrates this compartment and there is no direct access to the surface. The slightest stirring of the thick layers of silt found in this compartment and throughout the wreck's interior will obliterate visibility. There are also several smaller compartments in the aft quarter of the wreck that require careful penetration techniques. Only properly trained divers should penetrate these areas. As the wreck deteriorates and opens up further however, the presence of penetrable areas is decreasing.

Photo Tips: Opportunities abound on this wreck for all lenses and camera systems. The ship's interior compartments with their numerous hatchways are excellent for working with a model. Each compartment offers varying light levels demanding different technical requirements and offering a variety of scenic environments.

Outside the ship, the bow section presents a dramatic image for the wide-angle, available light system. The bow, as well as the stern and sides of the vessel host an incredible array of macro possibilities. Invertebrates thrive on this wreck; there are legions of Spanish Shawl nudibranchs all in

The Santa Cruz minesweeper wreck is well known for its large population of jewel-colored nudibranchs.

differing sizes that can accommodate almost any extension tube. There are also Hermissenda nudibranchs, navanax, and colorful spotted-rose anemo-

Drawing of the Winfield Scott leaving New York Harbor. Courtesy San Francisco Maritime Museum.

nes. Subject material is so profuse that photographers should consider taking two or more camera systems on each dive.

15. Winfield Scott

Depth to top:	20'	**Built:**	1850
Depth to bottom:	30'	**Sunk:**	1853
Average visibility:	30'	**Cause:**	Struck pinnacle and grounded
Expertise:	Novice	**Type:**	Side-wheel steamship
Current/surge:	Slight	**Length/Beam:**	225'/34'
Bottom:	Rocky reef	**Tonnage:**	1291
Location:	Anacapa Island	**Condition:**	Scattered wreckage remaining

History: The side-wheel steamship Winfield Scott was launched in New York on October 27, 1850. She was named after the renowned General Winfield Scott who was then the Commanding General of the U.S. Army.

The Scott was operated by the Vanderbilt Independent Line, and put into service on the busy Panama-San Francisco run.

After arriving in Panama two months late on her inaugural voyage, the Scott quickly became known as one of the finest steamships of its time on the gold rush route.

She generally accommodated between five and six hundred passengers in first, second, and steerage classes. Her 96-foot-long dining room allowed 100 passengers to eat at the same time. A large drawing room was furnished with sofas and chairs and handsomely decorated. Tickets for passage on the Scott ranged from $350 to $200 depending on class. Although the Scott was profitable, Vanderbilt sold her to the Pacific Mail Steamship Line.

Sinking: Departing San Francisco on December 3, 1853, the Winfield Scott was piloted by Captain Simon Blunt. Sailing down the coast in extremely heavy fog, the steamer approached the Channel Islands. Thinking his vessel to be in the channel between Anacapa and Santa Cruz Island, Captain Blunt continued southward, unconcerned about the lack of visibility.

With a sudden, violent lurch, the Scott came to a dead stop, her bow jammed against a rocky pinnacle. Water quickly began to pour inside through a large rip in her forward hold. Captain Blunt ordered engines reversed, but in backing off, her rudder struck another submerged reef. Rendered unnavigable, the Scott drifted helplessly in the shallows near Anacapa Island. Soon the swells pushed her onto the rocks a third time. This time the Scott stuck fast.

When the grounding occurred, it was late at night and panicked passengers rushed onto the deck. Fearing the Scott to be sinking, a group of men rushed the life boats, only to be held at bay by the revolvers of Captain Blunt and his officers. Before long, order was restored as the passengers realized that the ship was not in danger of sinking immediately. Soon a boat was lowered to find a suitable landing place ashore. As light approached, passengers, some provisions, mail, and a transport of gold was ferried to a deserted beach on Anacapa Island. Groundswells continued to batter the steamer as the marooned passengers and crew prepared to settle down for a long, cold wait.

The day after the grounding, coastal pioneer and island resident George Nidever landed at the site and loaned the castaways a supply of fishing tackle so they could augment their rationed diet with bounty from the sea.

Robbery soon became a problem, forcing the passengers to convene a committee of investigation which searched all personal belongings. A substantial amount of property was recovered and two thieves were flogged.

A week after the grounding, the steamship California was hailed by a cannon salvaged from the dying Scott. Unable to transport all the passengers, the California took aboard the women and children. On December 11 the Republic picked up the remaining castaways and delivered them to San Francisco.

The Dive: The wreck of the Winfield Scott is now over 135 years old and the forces of time have taken their toll. Consequently, little remains of the Scott today. The lack of large structures does not make the Scott a boring dive. Divers can hunt for shipbuilding clues now firmly attached to the rocky bottom and try to piece together a picture puzzle of the wreck. Side-wheel spokes play out a circular pattern in the rocky substrate. Portions of the large hub that once rolled her massive side-wheel still sit on the rocky bottom, as do scattered sheets of copper sheathing, pieces of iron, and splintered deck planks. Occasionally brass fastening spikes are seen. The wreckage is strewn throughout the shallows, continually covered or uncovered by sand during winter storms.

The jagged pinnacle that delivered the fatal blow to the Scott's bow can still be seen. The area is ringed by a thick kelp bed which gives way to sand in deeper water.

A diver descends on the Winfield Scott's sidewheel.

Perfume bottle found on the wreck of the Winfield Scott.

Artifacts: Since the steamer carried an unspecified amount of gold, the Winfield Scott has been scoured by treasure hunters with the hope that not all was removed when the vessel was wrecked. Major salvage operations occurred on the site in 1894, when the engines were dynamited loose and large amounts of copper and brass fastenings were recovered. During World War II, more copper and brass was removed for wartime scrap.

In the ensuing years sport divers have recovered bottles, dishes, and old coins, including several gold ones. Today, the wreck is protected by the National Park Service and no artifacts may be lawfully removed.

Hazards: During periods of large swells divers should be cautious of the accompanying surge which can slam them into one of the few remaining iron structures. Boaters should use caution when anchoring on the site due to the presence of sharp pinnacles, including the one which wrecked the Scott.

Photo Tips: With few large, dramatic structures and very little colorful invertebrate life, the Winfield Scott is not a photogenic wreck. However, wide-angle photographers may find some historical interest in the sidewheel remains.

4

Los Angeles County

16. Star of Scotland

Depth to top:	60'	**Built:**	1918
Depth to bottom:	75'	**Sunk:**	1942
Average visibility:	10'	**Cause:**	Hull plate leakage
Expertise:	Advanced	**Type:**	Q-boat (freighter)
Current/surge:	Minimal	**Length/Beam:**	400'
Bottom:	Silt	**Tonnage:**	Approximately 3500
Location:	Santa Monica Bay	**Condition:**	Breaking up

History: The Star of Scotland was originally commissioned HMS Mistletoe in 1918 by the British Royal Navy. The Mistletoe was a warship

A WWI "Q Boat" similar to the Star of Scotland, shown off Malta. Photograph from British Imperial War Museum.

cleverly disguised to resemble a freighter. These Q-ships, as they were called, would act as bait to lure German submarines into attacking.

Unbeknownst to the Germans, the facades on the main decks concealed a Pandora's box of heavy artillery. As the submarine approached on the surface, men aboard the Q-ships would run about wildly as if abandoning ship, and if under attack would light smudgepots to simulate damage. Once the submarine was close enough the trap was sprung. Down would come the phony bulwarks and out would come the guns, blasting away with deadly efficiency.

At the close of the war the Mistletoe was sold, renamed Chiapas, and used to haul passengers and produce between South America and the United States. Soon afterwards she changed hands again and, as La Playa Ensenada, worked the Mexican coast as a banana freighter. Later she moved to Baja California, was renamed La Playa, and operated as a gambling ship. Vessels of this nature were popular during Prohibition, allowing Americans to cross the Mexican border for an evening of drinking and gambling on a "cruise to nowhere." She was later renamed the City of Panama under Panamanian registry.

The former Q-ship quickly became a vessel of many identities. In the 1930s, under the new name of Star of Hollywood, the ship arrived in Santa Monica Bay and began operating locally as a floating casino, taking passengers beyond territorial limits for an evening of vice and gambling. Next the ship became the Texas, and was moored in Los Angeles harbor for several years, occasionally exiting for a gambling junket as well. In 1939 seagoing gambling ships became illegal along the California coast; the vessel's illicit days were over.

Captain Charles S. Arnold gave the ship her last name, the Star of Scotland, when he leased her. Captain Arnold and his wife lived aboard the ship and refurbished her as a fishing barge and nightclub. Dance floors and plush staterooms were added and large fishing stages were attached to her sides. Unfortunately, years of misuse and lack of maintenance, combined with the ship's age, began to show their effects. The once proud warship was now deteriorating badly.

Sinking: Shortly before 4 a.m. on January 23, 1942, a signal flare shot from the Star and burst in the night sky, illuminating the waters of Santa Monica Bay. Captain Arnold's crew had been fighting a losing battle all night against persistent leaks in the hullplates. The Star had been in need of repair for a long time and the hastily-applied cement patches were only a stopgap measure. Additional pumps had been placed aboard to keep the vessel afloat.

Two miles away on Santa Monica Pier lifeguards responded to the distress signal. The rescue boat arrived just in time to watch the large ship plunge beneath the surface stern first. One crew member died in the sinking. The ship's owner, Harry Wilson, and three crew members were taken to safety.

Inside the Star of Scotland's silt-covered hull, many holds and hatchways still await the skilled penetration diver.

The Dive: Getting a good dive on the Star is always an uncertain proposition. Visibility in the polluted Santa Monica Bay varies substantially, but is generally in the 10-foot range.

The monolithic lines of the 400-foot Star of Scotland rise high over the silt and rocks. Though she suffered slight damage when explosive charges were used to blow off her masts (which were a navigation hazard), the remaining structures are quite large.

Years later, a subsequent explosion by salvors destroyed portions of the wheelhouse. Today the wreck has become a haven for marine life. Divers will discover many large scallops and varieties of colorful invertebrates. Large fish school throughout the wreckage and lobster antennae are occasionally found sticking out from beneath rusting iron plates lying on the silty bottom.

Artifacts: Since poor visibility often renders the Star of Scotland undivable, many artifacts are still present. In the past when divers got an exceptional day, the Star produced cups and plates as well as several portholes.

At one time two enterprising salvors attempted to bring up the ship's wheel. After removing the artifact, they were unable to fit it through the small hatchway where lift bags were ready to bring the prize to the surface. The divers returned later with explosives to blow the hatchway apart. They miscalculated and used an excessive amount which blew off the bridge and sent the ship's wheel to oblivion at the same time.

Hazards: When diving the Star of Scotland, it's what a diver cannot see that can be harmful. The wreck is littered with monofilament fishing line and nets that have snagged on it over the years. To avoid entanglement dive cautiously, and avoid the Star altogether when visibility is poor. Always carry a sharp knife.

Divers should also be wary of heavy boat traffic and be sure to stay with the anchor line to and from the wreck.

Polluted water can be a concern as well. Check to be sure the City of Los Angeles has not dumped a million or so gallons of raw sewage into the Bay on the same day you plan your dive.

Photo Tips: Wide-angle photography has limited uses in poor visibility. But occasionally surprises can be in store, with enough clarity and ambient light to accommodate 15mm lenses. The good news is that the Star is a consistent producer of excellent close-up subject material. The shipwreck is heavily encrusted with marine invertebrates, offering extension tube photographers an abundance of subject choices. Divers will encounter throngs of starfish, anemones, and colorful filter-feeding animals. Those seeking photographs of fish will not be disappointed either. Large lingcod, bass and sheepshead frequent the site, as well as schools of blacksmith and perch.

Orange gorgonians and pink and white corynactis anemones grow over the former "submarine killer."

56

The great white steamship Avalon, off Casino Point, Catalina Island. Photograph courtesy of the Los Angeles Maritime Museum.

17. Avalon

Depth to top:	70'	**Built:**	1891
Depth to bottom:	85'	**Sunk:**	July, 1960
Average visibility:	20' to 30'	**Cause:**	Foundered in storm
Expertise:	Intermediate to advanced	**Type:**	3 deck passenger steamer
Current/surge:	Slight	**Length/Beam:**	264'/38'
Bottom:	Rocky reef	**Tonnage:**	1985
Location:	½ mile off Margate Street, Palos Verdes	**Condition:**	Shattered and strewn

History: The Avalon was built in 1891 at the Globe Iron Works Company in Cleveland, Ohio. Designed for use as a passenger steamer on the Great Lakes, she featured triple decks, large parlors, and elegant furnishings. Her high-nosed bow, 264-foot length and 38-foot beam added stature and regality to her already noble lines.

Originally named the S.S. Virginia, she ferried passengers from Chicago to Milwaukee. The ship was commandeered by the U.S. Navy during World War I. She was cut in half and towed through the canal system to the Atlantic where she was rewelded, converted to a troop transport, and renamed the

U.S.S. Blue Ridge. The ship never saw duty, however, as the war ended while she was still being refitted.

In 1919, she was purchased by chewing gum tycoon and owner of the Chicago Cubs, William Wrigley. Wrigley owned much of Catalina Island, which was enjoying a heyday as a West Coast resort. The steamer was brought through the Panama Canal and placed into service ferrying passengers from Los Angeles to Catalina Island. Wrigley renamed his vessel after the resort town of Avalon, located on the island.

Passengers boarded the "great white steamship" at a ferry terminal located at the foot of 6th street in San Pedro, now the site of the Los Angeles Maritime Museum. Revelers would dance their way across the channel to the popular big band tunes of the day. On holidays and weekends, the ship featured its own orchestra.

When World War II broke out, the Avalon ferried servicemen to the training station located on the island. Once the war was over the Avalon found herself in the passenger trade again. By 1951, smaller, faster, and more cost-effective vessels had entered the island transit trade and the Avalon was retired. A grand, colorful era had come to a close.

The Avalon languished at anchor inside Los Angeles harbor for nine years until she was purchased by an Oregon lumber firm. The Avalon's new owners removed much of the upper portion of the vessel for salvage and converted the hull into a lumber barge.

Sinking: It was in this new condition that the Avalon was towed northward up the Palos Verdes coast en route to the forests of the Pacific Northwest. With a large salvage crane on her stern deck, and her hull cut practically to the waterline, she was ungainly at best. Moving past Rocky Point, the Avalon foundered in a storm and sank. Although it was rumored that the ship was purposely scuttled to collect insurance money, nothing conclusive was proven. The Avalon broke in half and settled to the bottom in 85 feet of water. Her once noble bow is still recognizable though it now rests upside down.

The Dive: Be forewarned: the Avalon can be elusive. Over the years, storms have flattened the wreck below the height of the finger reefs that surround her. Though difficult to locate with a depth finder and loran, most local charter boat captains can place divers on the wreck with little difficulty.

Descending to her silt-covered decks, divers will quickly discover that there is still a lot left of the old steamship and that considerable time is needed to swim her whole length. Brass plumbing fixtures protrude from the collapsed piles of iron and steel. Kelpbass, sheepshead, and blacksmith congregate over these metallic reefs. Rockfish and lingcod lurk beneath rusting hull plates.

The crane that made the Avalon's last voyage lies flipped over next to the stern, looking curiously out of place with its myriad gears and pulleys.

Gears from the Avalon's crane now lie on their sides, covered with algae and starfish.

Small schools of perch swim in and out of its cab.

Divers can enter what is left of the bow and stern sections of the Avalon, and peer inside cavernous fuel bunkers as well. The vertical bow section is still easily recognizable. The high, blunt lines are hard to miss as they clearly typify the marine architecture of the period. This forward area is heavily populated with colorful starfish and bright gorgonians that present a dazzling display of pinks, yellows, oranges, and greens.

Red and pink corynactis anemones dot the whole area. Bass and Garibaldi dart through collapsed companionways. Occasional tell-tale lobster antennae protrude from underneath pieces of wreckage, making the Avalon a popular site among underwater hunters. Nudibranch seekers will almost always encounter a thriving contingent of Spanish shawl.

The water temperature on the Avalon is always a bit chilly, even during summer months. A noticeable thermocline is invariably present, and one advantage of this is that the water at depth is usually very clear, regardless of surface conditions.

Artifacts: Some would describe this wreck as having been ''picked over,'' for there are few recoverable artifacts readily visible. But then as always, looks can be deceiving. Experienced divers know that ''picked over'' wrecks can still yield surprises. In past years divers exploring debris pockets have uncovered items such as old coins, stateroom keys, brass fittings, and other marine hardware.

The Avalon's wheel and telegraph are on display at the Avalon Museum on Catalina Island where nautical enthusiasts can view them as well as other memorabilia from the ship's past.

The Avalon is well known for the colorful gorgonians that drape the bow and smaller penetrable areas.

Hazards: Because of the 80-foot depth and colder water, it is a good idea to use a slightly more conservative dive plan and to monitor your air closely.

Photo Tips: The Avalon presents photographers with a variety of opportunities. The larger remaining structures, especially the bow and the crane operator's cab, offer interesting angles for a 15mm lens. The bow section hosts many invertebrate subjects such as starfish, gorgonians, and anemones. The crane arm is usually filled with schools of small fish cruising through its lattice-like structure. Many bottom-dwelling fish can be found hiding in darker holds and crevices, presenting easy targets for the stalking cameraman.

18. Dominator

Depth to top:	partially out of water	**Built:**	1945
Depth to bottom:	25'	**Sunk:**	March 13, 1961
Average visibility:	5' to 15'	**Cause:**	Ran aground
Expertise:	Advanced	**Type:**	Liberty Ship/ Freighter
Current/surge:	Surge can be severe	**Length/Beam:**	441' (length)
Bottom:	Rocky reef	**Tonnage:**	10,000
Location:	Rocky Point, Palos Verdes	**Condition:**	Badly ripped and strewn

History: The Dominator was one of the many Liberty ships mass-produced during World War II to provide the transport needed to supply our allies. After the war, most of these vessels were sold and used as grainers, colliers, or freighters. Some were sold to shipping barons such as Aristotle Onassis, thus many former Liberty Ships ended up in Greek registry. One such ship was named the Dominator.

In the spring of 1961, the Dominator called at Vancouver, British Columbia to pick up a 9,000-ton load of grain. Captained by Charitos Papanikolpulos, the ship was due for a short refueling stop at Los Angeles harbor, and then bound for Algiers to offload its cargo valued at one million dollars.

On Monday, March 13, 1961, Captain Papanikolpulos' ship moved slowly along the Southern California coast. He knew Los Angeles harbor was only a few minutes away, but was encountering a slight problem. He was surrounded by a blanket of pea-soup fog. So the large ship inched its way south.

Slightly before 6 pm the relatively quiet community of Palos Verdes Estates echoed with an eerie screeching and grating sound throughout its foggy hillsides. Numerous calls were made to the local police department as concerned residents wondered what the mysteriously frightening sound could be. As Lieutenant Buck Dollarhide arrived on the scene, he took one look over the cliff at Rocky Point and radioed, "Boy, we're going to have a problem here." What the Lieutenant saw was the huge freighter perched on an offshore reef. He knew that the normally quiet Palos Verdes community and its newly acquired shipwreck would be the focus of media attention throughout the nation.

He underestimated slightly. Upon report of the stranding, news services quickly began flashing photographs of the stranded Dominator from New York to Tokyo.

Sinking: As members of the press and curiosity seekers flocked to the hillside estates of Palos Verdes Peninsula, the Dominator held firmly to the rocky reef it had impaled itself upon. Captain Papanikolpulos attempted to back the ship off at high tide with its own engines, but the 441-foot vessel remained stuck 100 yards from shore. Later, hundreds gathered atop the 80-foot cliff at Rocky Point to watch a Smith Rice Company super-derrick barge attempt to wrest the Dominator from shore. As the Dominator's captain and crew watched from the deck of the ship, the barge managed to pull the vessel about ten feet before giving up.

The Dominator ruptured hullplates at 3 holds when she hit the reef, leaving the inner holds and cargo untouched for the time being. By the fourth day of her stranding, extremely high seas and fierce winds buffeted the ship. That night the captain radioed for help, "Dominator breaking up. Master requests assistance." Due to the heavy seas and loss of light, the Coast Guard delayed rescue operations until morning.

When dawn came, 15-foot-waves were battering the vessel. Two Coast Guard cutters stood by while a landing craft maneuvered to the leeward side of the ship, which had now become a foaming iron seawall. As spray crested the top of the bridge, the crew scampered down a rope ladder into the rescue craft. The master and his officers remained aboard.

The Dominator's hull slowly began to break up, allowing seawater to mix into the cargo hold full of grain. The expanding grain caused the heavy iron plates to buckle and blow apart at their welds. It was at this time that Captain Papanikolpulos and his officers decided that they too, should abandon ship. The Coast Guard responded again, and removed the remaining castaways.

Some time later, would-be salvors and adventure seekers swam out to the hulk. Several boarded the Dominator and claimed the wreck their own by right of possession. As night began to fall and seas grew large and rough once again, the would-be salvors decided to abandon ship as well. Several jumped into the swirling waters and were instantly caught by fierce currents and waves. Those that remained on the ship were rescued by a Marine Corps Helicopter. As the chopper pulled the last scavenger off the ship, a huge wave hit the aircraft broadside, forcing the pilot to go into a steep climb as the rescue victim dangled at the end of a cable. The adventurers were all arrested once ashore for interfering with a disaster in progress.

As time wore on the stubborn ship began to deteriorate. Only a partial load of grain was eventually salvaged. Later, as authorized salvors began removing portions of the Dominator's superstructure, a welding torch spark caused a five hour blaze that blackened the ship. While the remaining grain rotted in the holds, Palos Verdes residents were confronted with a new problem other than throngs of onlookers; thousands of black flies swarmed to the ship, attracted by the smell of rotting grain. Finally, after being battered for months, the Dominator succumbed to the sea and waves and broke in half, sending much of her structure plummeting to the shallow depths. All that currently remains of the Dominator at the surface are pieces of jagged metal that protrude from the waterline at low tide, and a portion of the bow which has been tossed up on the beach.

The Dive: Today the Dominator is only a shattered image of her once massive self. The forces of time and the sea have ripped her apart and strewn her pieces in such a violent tumult that the dive site area containing her wreckage resembles an underwater junkyard. Her wreckage lies from the shoreline at Rocky Point outward toward the reef that doomed her. Wreckage is scattered in an area up to 35 feet deep. The Dominator is a shallow water wreck, meaning she can only be dived on extremely calm days. When surf pounds the shoreline, surge can become quite severe. This action, combined with all of her jagged metal and rusting machinery means that divers should always carefully consider the ocean conditions when planning a dive on the Dominator.

When the sea is cooperative however, the Dominator makes an interesting shallow water wreck dive. The wreck site itself has become a thriving reef, covered with a lush kelp bed. This means that divers should forget any notion of snorkeling out to the wreck. The thickness of the kelp growth is such that surface swimmers would have difficulty in making any progress. Divers must navigate to the wreck site from outside the underwater kelp. Natural navigational techniques are important as the large amounts of metal present render a compass useless. Once divers have accessed the wreck area, the powerful testimony of the sea's force becomes quickly evident. Huge twisted iron plates, smashed bulkheads, and rearranged boilers lie opened along the bottom like empty tin cans. The sea claimed the wreck quickly; the thick kelp forest has all but transformed the wreck into an undersea hanging garden. Surge is almost always present, although a relaxed, experienced diver should have little difficulty negotiating its pull and pushing action. Divers will encounter less surge on the deeper portions of the wreck.

Even though the ship has been heavily battered against the bottom, there is still much to see. Massive pieces of the engines and boilers can be found at 20 feet, and iron hull and deckplates lie tossed atop the reef like children's toys. There are even sections of companionways remaining. Divers penetrating these long, narrow corridors have been known to encounter large spiny lobster in the farthest recesses. Most of the wreckage is covered with a heavy green growth of algae. Bright orange Garibaldi dart in and out of their lairs throughout the wreck.

Artifacts: The Dominator has seen many salvage attempts since her sinking in 1961. The adventuresome band of young men who attempted to claim the wreck as their own several days after the ship ran aground managed to remove the wheel and binnacle from the bridge, although they were unable

A diver examines one of the Dominator's doors.

to swim their treasure to shore. Sport divers have been a bit more successful over the years. Since surge and surf conditions do not allow the Dominator to be dived every day of the week, there are still many goodies to be found on her. Over the years divers have recovered brass valves, pieces of porcelain, and bulkhead doors.

Hazards: Sharp, jagged remnants of twisted iron and steel, combined with strong surge, can present serious problems for divers visiting the Dominator. Consequently the wreck should only be dived on the calmest of days. For divers lacking experience in California kelp diving, the thick surface kelp canopy can be a problem as well. While the Dominator is accessible from shore, a boat is still the best recommendation. To reach the site on the beach it is necessary for divers to negotiate a slippery trail down an 80-foot cliff and then walk down the boulder-strewn beach to Rocky Point. As soon as divers enter the water, the kelp bed begins. Generally speaking, a boat entry is far less arduous.

Photo Tips: When visibility is limited, the Dominator can be less than a tremendously photogenic wrecksite. The larger remaining structures do provide interesting material for wider angle systems if the diver can hold his ground in the surge long enough to take a shot. Since the Dominator rests in the surge zone, some invertebrate life has been slow to take to the algae-covered iron plates and beams. For these reasons the Dominator is not well known for its macro photography.

The de-masted fishing barge Olympic. Courtesy California Wreck Divers.

19. Olympic

Depth to top:	75'	**Built:**	1877
Depth to bottom:	100'	**Sunk:**	1940
Average visibility:	12–20'	**Cause:**	Rammed by freighter
Expertise:	Intermediate to advanced	**Type:**	3 masted barkentine
Current:	0 to 2 knots, surge during large swell	**Length/Beam:**	320'/38'
Bottom:	Sand with reef	**Tonnage:**	1569
Location:	4 miles off L.A. Harbor Lighthouse	**Condition:**	Twisted amidships, but partially intact

History: The 1,569 ton squared-rigged barkentine, Star of France slid off the ways at the famous shipyard of Harland and Wolff in Belfast, Ireland in 1877. She and her sister ship, the Star of Italy were built for Irish merchant J. P. Corry, and consigned to serve in the jute trade between Britain and India. Although their tonnage and length were not as large as some contemporary clippers of the day, with lower and topmasts joined together the ships were very tall and afforded plenty of sail. These iron-hulled barks set several speed records and were the fastest Harland & Wolff clippers in Corry's fleet. The Star of France's best recorded time was 93 days from Calcutta to London in 1883. In 1897 she sailed from London to San Francisco in 113 days. Due to her speed and ability to hold a cargo of 2,250 tons, the Star of France was a valuable transport in the Corry fleet where quickness on the water and quantity in the hold gave his ships a competitive edge. In later years, the Star moved out of the jute business into regular colonial trade in the North and South Pacific.

J.J. Moore & Co. purchased the ship in 1898 and transferred it to Hawaiian registry. Later in 1905, the Star passed into the hands of the Alaska Packers Company, where she was refitted and began a new career ferrying men and machinery along the rugged Pacific Northwest coast. She also served as a floating salmon-packing ship. As sailing vessels began to fade into obscurity, the Star changed ownership again. In 1934 she was purchased by captain J. M. Anderson of the Hermosa Beach Amusement Company. The ship's elegant masts were cut to the first crosstees and her name was changed to Olympic. She was towed from San Francisco to Long Beach where much of her rigging was removed. She soon found herself tied up to her permanent mooring outside Los Angeles Harbor where she was to serve as a fishing barge—a sad end for the once proud and graceful sailing ship.

The Olympic was employed in its new capacity for six years. A coffee shop-restaurant was placed aboard. Anglers could secure sleeping accommodations and actually spend several days at anchor fishing the nearby reefs that were very productive for rockfish and lingcod. By all appearances the Olympic settled nicely into her new duty.

Sinking: Business came to an abrupt halt for the Olympic early in the morning on September 4, 1940. A thick fog had blanketed the area, obscuring visibility. Two tugboats had just pulled alongside the barge when suddenly the bow of the Japanese freighter Sakito Maru appeared through the gloom and slammed into the ship's port side. Since the Olympic was permanently moored, the two ships stuck together and little water entered. A few moments after the collision however, the captain of the Sakito reversed engines. This error in seamanship exposed a cavernous breech and water cascaded inside the fishing barge. The Olympic sank within minutes, taking four passengers and three crew to the bottom in 100 feet of water. Shortly after the sinking, several hard hat divers visited the ship to set explosive charges that would release any bodies trapped inside her shattered hull. All bodies of victims were eventually recovered. Seventeen people were rescued immediately after she went down.

Alone in her watery grave, the Olympic faded into obscurity until almost two decades later when an unfortunate purse seiner snagged onto it, interpreting its large mass on the depth recorder as a large school of fish. A short time later a young man named Roy Hauser (who now operates the west coast dive boats, Truth, Conception, and Vision) floated the first marker on the wreck site. The long lost Olympic had been rediscovered.

The Dive: In her days as a clipper ship, the Star/Olympic was larger than life, full of color and adventure. Today as a shipwreck, she remains the same. Divers venturing down the anchorline through 100 feet of blue-green water will find that she still has much to offer. The hull of the ship is relatively intact, although rather shattered and twisted amidships where demolition occurred after the sinking. The bow section tilts toward the sand bottom with a severe starboard list. The midships area is relatively level. The mammoth stern section rises high off the sand bottom and tilts to starboard as well. To gain full view of this large ship in its perspective requires at least two dives. Wooden decking has long since rotted away (although storms occasionally uncover some preserved teakwood), revealing a barren hull with empty crisscrossing beams that divers can swim between. These iron girders are especially noticeable on the bow and stern sections and are heavily encrusted with brilliant pink corynactis anemones, orange mantled scallops and a variety of invertebrates in dazzling blue, green, and yellow hues.

Fish school through the Olympic's bow beams and girders.

The shipwreck's biggest attraction is fish. Throngs of bass, perch, and blacksmith school over the site. Divers descending onto the site usually pass through a large congregation of fish before they see the wreck itself. On the wreck, cabezon, sculpin, and lingcod can be found lying atop the rusting beams and bulwarks. Sheepshead and calico bass warily cruise the darker holds. Divers venturing inside some of the semi- penetrable areas will often surprise sleeping gamefish. Off in the distant bluewater, large pelagic jellyfish, mola mola, and the occasional skipjack swim by.

Encrusted machinery lies atop the Olympic's decks. Huge bitts are still securely bolted into the rails. Lengths of anchorchain are dumped into confused patterns along the bottom. The massive bowsprit stretches out over the sand, pointing off into the neighboring reef formations in the hazy distance. Due to the wreck's close proximity to Los Angeles harbor, the site is visited regularly by sport divers. The Olympic offers tremendous wreck diving excitement only a short boat ride from port.

Artifacts: The wreck has given up many treasures over the years. Portholes, the ship's bell, wheel, and binnacle cover have all been raised by pioneering wreck divers in the early 60s and 70s. In 1972 a local club,

"Alaskan Packer's" porthole from the Olympic/Star of France.

the California Wreck Divers, salvaged the ship's 2 ton capstan using six 50 gallon drums and pneumatic tools. The capstan was donated to the Los Angeles Maritime Museum. Teak planking, cage lamps, and belaying pins have all surfaced from the old windjammer over the years.

Even though the Olympic is what many old timers still consider to be "a picked-over wreck," unexpected prizes continue to be discovered. Recently, large storms have swept her clean, removing years of sediment from inside her hull. For a time antique bottles, china plates, cups, and bowls were recovered. Several Golden State Dairy fluted milk bottles with dates stamped on the bottom have come off the wreck as well.

Hazards: Probably the major hazard when diving the Olympic has to do with the reason she went down in the first place; shipping. She sits directly in front of Los Angeles harbor. Large naval vessels, freighters, supertankers, and colliers still ply the waters over the Olympic. It is always advisable to dive the wreck only on clear days when diver down flags can be readily seen by incoming traffic.

It is important that divers descend and ascend while using the anchorline as a reference. Strong currents can also rip through over the site. A properly placed anchorline can prevent divers from being blown off course when descending. There is also a large amount of netting draped over the wreck itself, which can create possible entanglement problems. Divers are advised to carry a sharp knife and avoid stumbling into the netting.

Finally, the depth of the wreck presents problems of its own. Divers must pay close attention to depth and time limitations. Air supply is more limited at 100 feet so careful monitoring of air consumption is critical. Spearfishing is generally discouraged on the wreck due to the rapid consumption of air involved.

Photo Tips: The Olympic presents tremendous opportunities to all underwater photographers. The concentration of colorful marine invertebrates affords macro photographers a field day. Brightly colored anemone and nudibranch populations pose endless possibilities for extension tube and reflex macro systems. Throngs of fish teeming through the structures of the ship also present splendid backdrops for the wide-angle connoisseur. Close-up photography is a sure bet on the Olympic, even if visibility is marginal. Wide angle photography can be a little more chancy due to available light and water clarity; but a lot of times the visibility gets surprisingly good (in the 30' to 80' range!). The best structures offering varieties of subject material are found on the bow and stern sections—but keep your eyes open! Great possibilities are found throughout the entire wreck.

20. The Valiant

Depth to top:	80'	**Built:**	1926
Depth to bottom:	100'	**Sunk:**	1930
Average visibility:	30' to 60'	**Cause:**	Fire and explosion
Expertise:	Intermediate to advanced	**Type:**	Motor yacht
Current/surge:	Minimal	**Length/Beam:**	147' (length)
Bottom:	Silt and sand	**Tonnage:**	440 tons
Location:	Descanso Bay, Catalina Island	**Condition:**	Partially intact, but breaking up

History: Built by the Newport News Shipping and Drydock Company, the yacht Valiant was one of the largest private vessels of its kind in U.S. Registry. It was custom-constructed in 1926 at a cost of $750,000 for Maine millionaire Hugh J. Chisholm. The Valiant was the first American vessel made with a double bottom for storage of fuel and water. Not only was the design an efficient use of storage space, it also provided the vessel with better stability at sea. Two enormous diesel engines powered the yacht, enabling it to cruise at the brisk clip of 18 knots. A complement of twenty men served aboard the luxurious vessel. Chisholm christened the vessel Aras (his wife's name spelled backwards). The ship was later purchased by Charles Howard, owner of the Howard Motor Company.

Mr. and Mrs. Howard and crew sailed the yacht through the Panama Canal and throughout the South Pacific. In addition to operating the west coast's only Buick distributorship, Mr. Howard was also a trustee of the San Francisco Museum. While visiting the Pacific islands he collected native artifacts for display in San Francisco. Prior to his journey, Mr. Howard had a gasoline-driven motor installed in the engine room to power the ship's auxiliary generator more quietly. The new system spared the passengers from the constant noisy rumblings of the diesel-driven powerplant. The new engine however, would later prove to be the Valiant's demise.

Sinking: It was evening, December 13, 1930, as the 147' palatial yacht rested at anchor in Catalina Island's Descanso Bay. The Valiant had called earlier at Los Angeles harbor to take on visiting friends for a brief cruise to Catalina. The Howards were on the last leg of their Pacific odyssey and were soon to return to San Francisco. Mr. and Mrs. Howard were in the main salon entertaining guests while dinner was being prepared in the galley. Passengers relaxed as strains of popular music floated over the water.

The Valiant's lights blazed brightly in the night sky, flickered, then abruptly went out. A crew member grabbed a flashlight and ran to the Valiant's engine room. The gasoline-driven generator had run dry. Opening the valve, he started a flow of gas from the storage tank to the smaller generator tank. After the engine restarted, the lights and music came back on and the crewman returned to his quarters—without shutting off the main fuel tank's gas line. Hundreds of gallons of volatile gasoline began to soak the engine room floor. Soon, a violent explosion rocked the engine room, setting the Valiant's midship section bursting into flames. The Valiant's captain was on the bridge at the time. The force of the explosion blew a door off its hinges and knocked him unconscious. In the galley, the ship's Filipino baker was at work until the blast ripped a deep hole in the floor. Falling into the chasm, he became trapped at chest level and began to scream. Hearing the man's cries for help, Mr. Howard rushed to the galley. He courageously extinguished the man's burning clothes and pulled him to safety, scalding his own hands badly in the process. Crew members carried their captain to a lifeboat while Mr. Howard calmly led his guests to the

The Valiant was a palatial yacht. Courtesy California Wreck Divers.

bow and loaded them into a launch also. A flotilla of small private craft raced from shore to the burning yacht to assist in taking on survivors. Eventually all crew members were taken to safety.

Roused from what would have been a routine watch, Avalon Harbormaster Francis McGrath soon found himself hard at work. Upon seeing the explosion, he too sped to the vessel and began picking up swimming crewmembers. Fearing more explosions that would imperil nearby vessels, McGrath attempted to tow the 147' floating bonfire out of the bay. Despite his efforts, subsequent explosions dropped the Valiant's stern anchor into the water, deploying lengths of chain that stranded the vessel within the bay. All the harbormaster could do was cast off and let the yacht burn.

The fire raged uncontrollably for three days, fed by thousands of gallons of diesel oil from the ship's main fuel bunkers. As the flames subsided and the ship cooled down, steel plates riveted to the Valiant's hull shrank. Water quickly poured inside and she sank within minutes, plunging 100 feet to the bottom.

The Dive: Today the Valiant sits upright on the sandy bottom. Her bow is posed at 100 feet, facing open sea. The stern rests near Descanso Bay at 85 feet. Much of her superstructure deteriorated quickly after the explosion and fire, leaving only a cavernous, burned-out hull. Divers will encounter small shallow penetrable compartments along the bow, and astern. Strands of kelp grow along the Valiant's starboard side. To the undiscerning diver, the Valiant may not appear to be much of a wreck. But a closer look will reveal more than rusting iron plates. Colorful seafans and anemones grow along her sides. Schools of blacksmith, senorita, bass, and silvery baitfish embroil the rusting ribs and railings of the wreck. Lobster and eels lurk

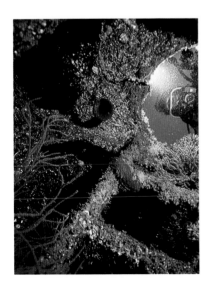

Ladder and hatch found within the Valiant's bow compartment.

The telegraph from the Valiant.

inside dark crevices. The ship's bow rises high above the silty sand bottom at 100 feet and lists slightly to port.

Divers exploring the ship will discover the remnants of the engine room area and the gasoline engine that ignited the Valiant's fatal spark. A high mound of debris is piled up amidships where divers will encounter sheets of crumbling iron, valves and pipe, and piles of rusting anchor chain. Fanning through the silt pockets divers will occasionally unearth artifacts from the Valiant's sinking almost 40 years ago.

As the effects of prolonged immersion wear on, the Valiant slowly continues to crumble and deteriorate. The good news for recreational divers is that much of her hull structure still remains, offering unique opportunities for photography, game collecting, and shipwreck exploration.

Artifacts: The Valiant has been the subject of much sport and commercial salvage over the years. In 1955 a team of salvors removed one of the ship's 70-inch bronze propellers, which weighed in near 1,000 pounds. The other prop had been taken off the previous week by famous treasure salvor Mel Fisher, who then owned Mel's Aqua Shop in Redondo Beach. But salvors haven't scoured the Valiant's grave for brass, bronze, and lead ballast only. Many have sought Mrs. Howard's lost pewter jewelry box, reportedly containing over $67,000 worth of diamonds and gems. To date, the box remains unrecovered (if anyone has found the jewels, they're not talking). Another small source of treasure that comes up from the Valiant from time to time are Mr. Howard's drink tokens. These small coins were labeled "Good for one drink" and bore the Valiant's name. Mr. Howard would negotiate a prior agreement with local tavern keepers so that his guests could use the tokens in bars. Before shipping off, Howard would visit the local watering holes and personally redeem his "Good for one drink" tokens.

72

Hazards: The only major consideration when diving the Valiant is depth. Because she rests in 100 feet of water, divers should take great care in monitoring their dive profiles and watching the air remaining in their pressure gauges. Divers should also note that the Valiant is accessible only during the fall, winter and spring months, as nearby Avalon Bay boat traffic can lend itself to hazardous surface conditions during the busy summer season. Permission to dive the wreck is required. Divers can obtain this by radioing the Avalon Harbormaster.

Photo Tips: Visibility is the main contributing factor to obtaining good photographs of the Valiant. Usually the water is quite clear on the wreck, although springtime plankton does reduce visibility. Wide angle photographers may want to swim to the sand at the front of the ship and photograph the large bow structure that looms off the bottom, as well as shoot the large schools of Spanish Mackerel that at times boil over the ship. Macro photographers will find colorful seafans and stone corals growing throughout the site.

21. The SueJac

Depth to top:	70'	**Built:**	1968
Depth to bottom:	90'	**Sunk:**	1980
Average visibility:	40' to 80'	**Cause:**	Driven onto breakwater during high winds
Expertise:	Novice to intermediate	**Type:**	Ferro-cement sailboat
Current/surge:	Minimal	**Length/Beam:**	65' (length)
Bottom:	Breakwater rocks sloping to sand	**Tonnage:**	Unknown
Location:	Casino Point Breakwater, Avalon, Catalina Island (underneath extreme southern buoy marking Avalon's Underwater Park)	**Condition:**	Deteriorating

History: The 65' schooner-rigged sailing ship SueJac was built in Puget Sound in 1968. The SueJac was a ferro-cement boat, its hull constructed from a conglomeration of chicken wire, water piping, lightweight steel bars and cement.

Ferro-cement vessels are a relatively revolutionary type of water craft. The new technology and simple methods of construction offer boat builders an economic alternative to the most costly and traditional methods of marine architecture. Proponents of ferro-cement design state that the hull designs are fireproof, low in maintenance and extremely seaworthy.

The SueJac was constructed with the intent to actually appear older than she was. The vessel's interior featured decorative tiles and the exterior structures were made from hand-tooled wood, giving the boat a classic nautical style. In the fall of 1980 she was anchored outside of Avalon harbor, Catalina Island. The SueJac was provisioned for a 6-month cruise and carried a three man crew aboard. It was rumored however, that the crew was owed 4 months back wages by the owners.

Sinking: The elegant schooner became the unfortunate victim of Santa Ana winds blowing full force against Catalina Island. These strong northeasterly desert winds blow offshore from the mainland and buffet the usually placid lee side of the island. During these conditions, winds gusting up to 45 mph can create 5 to 6 foot breakers on shore. These wind-generated waves can smash against the port town of Avalon, creating havoc among pleasure craft not securely anchored inside the breakwater. It was during such a wild and windy episode that the cement-hulled SueJac, for some unknown reason, was anchored up outside of the Avalon breakwater.

Moorings were readily available inside while the cement boat kicked and bucked like a bronco at anchor. It was a chilly Saturday morning as wind lashed sheets of frigid water across the surface of Avalon harbor. At 7:30 the crew checked the SueJac's anchor and all was still well. At 9:30 a.m. however, the winds had increased considerably. Avalon Baywatch Lifeguards were cruising the harbor, making sure all boats were securely tied. At the same time, a short distance around the breakwater, the SueJac lost her hold on the bottom and began to drag anchor into Catalina's Underwater Park. The winds drove the sailboat against the rocks. She slammed into the rocks once, bounced off, and slammed into the rocks again. By this time, witnesses were watching the scene and signaled the Baywatch boat, which was a short distance away inside the harbor. The crew was still on the sailboat as it was carried towards the harbor entrance, threatening to slam into moored vessels inside. The wind blew the boat back onto the rocks a third time (outside of the Underwater Park boundary) and she quickly sank.

Lifeguard Dennis Zimmerman dove into the water, rescuing the three crew members and their dog. A single large crack in the port side dealt the sailboat its deathblow, sending the SueJac to the bottom within seconds, bow first.

The Dive: The SueJac can be slightly disorienting to those who dive her for the first time. She sits on a 45 degree angle, almost as if surfing down the breakwater wall, bow pointed to the bottom. Additionally, the boat lists radically to starboard. The confused angle of the wreck creates an imbalanced "funhouse" effect. This can cause a disorienting sensory change resulting in a slight vertigo experience in divers who drop down onto the sailboat for

The crack in the SueJac's ferrocement hull that sealed its fate on the Casino Point breakwater.

the first time. A lush kelp bed grows astern, shrouding the picturesque wreck in a forest of deep green and amber. The boat rests on a jumbled pile of rocks that flow downward from the breakwater. The entire wreck itself is easily penetrable. Divers can enter through the main hatchway located at the wheel cockpit in the stern and drop inside the cabin. Inside, divers will discover a variety of useless discarded junk, including electrical wiring and portions of the sailboat's engine. The ship's wheel has been removed along with most of its portholes. Moving forward, divers will find another large hatchway to swim through. Several feet in front of this is a smaller secondary hatch, but divers should avoid swimming through this one (you could get stuck!). The ship's mast and boom are long since gone. All that remains on the above decks are a few bent stainless steel railing posts. The sailboat's heavy concrete keel lies wedged along the rocky bottom.

Recent storms have battered the wreck severely. More decking and support structures have fallen off. If nature has its way, it appears that the Sue Jac will soon resemble a cavernous hulk.

Divers will discover the wreck to be home to many varieties of friendly fish. Since the wreck is within the protected confines of the Avalon Underwater Park, no game may be taken from the area. This makes the wreck area a prolific spot for marine life. Divers will encounter large calico bass, Garibaldi, sheepshead and varieties of small reef fish. With the kelp canopy above the wreck and the schools of fish throughout, the resting place of the SueJac is picturesque as well as interesting.

Artifacts: After the sailboat went down, divers flocked to the site and began removing anything of value left on her. Shortly after this, the boundaries of the Underwater Park at Avalon were extended to include the

Stacey Douglass swims inside the wreck's forward cabin.

wreck and portions of Casino Point. Because of this, no artifacts may currently be taken from the wreck site.

Hazards: Like the nearby Valiant, the SueJac has only a few potential problems associated with her. Depth is a major consideration. Divers should watch their available bottom time and air supply.

Since Casino Point is directly next to Avalon Harbor, boat traffic intensity can be a problem. Divers accessing the wreck from shore do so with relative safety as most boaters do not transgress the ropes and buoys marking the park's boundaries. Divers swimming to the park from a seaward vessel should make sure that "the coast is clear" to avoid being run down by passing vessels. Flying a diver down flag is a good idea, but few weekend sailors know what one means, so dive defensively!

Photo Tips: Probably the most interesting area to shoot photographs is the upward angle from inside the wreck. Ambient light streams down through the hatchway while the kelp glistens in the background overhead. A model poised at the entrance to the wreck can make for a striking shot. As water clarity is usually excellent in this area, a wide-angle system has some distinct advantages.

22. The Gregory

Depth to top:	breaks surface at low tide	**Built:**	1944
Depth to bottom:	20'	**Sunk:**	1972

Average visibility:	5' to 30'	**Cause:**	Aerial bombardment
Expertise:	Advanced	**Type:**	Destroyer
Current/surge:	Surge moderate to severe	**Length/Beam:**	376' (length)
Bottom:	Rocky reef & boulders	**Tonnage:**	2100 tons
Location:	On the beach at San Clemente Island between Mail & Lost Points	**Condition:**	Broken up

History: DD.802, the USS Gregory, was a "Later Fletcher" class destroyer. This particular group of Fletcher Class destroyers carried the "later" designation as 56 additional ships were ordered built in 1942. Considered to be the finest class of destroyers to serve in World War II, the Gregory and her sisters received their baptism of fire in the Pacific campaign.

Fletcher destroyers carried heavy anti-aircraft armament: five twin 40mm guns, and seven 20mm guns. Combined with the available complement of five 127mm guns (5"), four 28mm guns, torpedoes, and depth charges, the Fletchers were quick, effective killers as they engaged aircraft, ships, and submarines.

Launched in 1944, the Gregory began its tour of duty in time to participate in the amphibious assault on Iwo Jima. The Gregory provided support for landing marines and was under continual attack for over a month, giving her newly assembled crew little opportunity to catch their breaths. Her next assignment was during the invasion of Okinawa. While on radar picket patrol, the Gregory was attacked by three Kamikaze aircraft. Two were splashed by successful gunnery. The third, while receiving a hailstorm of anti-aircraft rounds managed to score a hit on the destroyer's midship section. Crewmen were able to prevent the ship from sinking as water poured inside her forward engine and fire rooms. Temporary repairs were made to keep the Gregory above water. Still damaged badly, she left Okinawa and steamed to San Diego. Three months later the war was over. The Gregory received 2 battle stars for its brief but effective role in the Pacific campaign.

In 1950, the Korean Conflict began and the Gregory was placed into action again. She spent 2 years patrolling the hostile Korean coast where she screened the carriers Essex and Boxer, which launched air strikes against North Korean positions. The Gregory was also frequently assigned to the Formosa Patrol. Her presence was intended to inhibit Communist aggression against the free Chinese Republic. In 1953, while on a search and rescue mission for a downed P2V, she came within 800 yards of Nan-ao Tao, a Communist-held island a short distance off the Chinese coast. The shore batteries opened fire, but the Gregory left the area to continue its rescue mission. During the Korean War, she received 4 more battle stars.

As part of the post-war Navy, the Gregory undertook training exercises off the California coast and was deployed six months of the year in the Far East. In the fall of 1958, the Gregory spent 2½ tension filled months off the Chinese coast during the Quemoy-Matsu crisis.

Sinking: The Gregory was decommissioned at San Diego on February 1, 1964 and entered the reserve. She was struck from the Navy List of Ships in 1966 and later served as a training ship in San Diego, assuming the name Indoctrinator. In 1972, the once-valiant warrior was towed to the backside of San Clemente Island between Mail Point and Lost Point. It was here that the Gregory was blown apart for target practice. She settled in shallow water, with portions of the vessel coming to rest ashore. The Gregory's bow and 5-inch gun ended up on the rocky beach. The shattered aft and midship sections run through the surfline and downward into 20 feet of water.

The Dive: Due to its close proximity to shore, the divable sections of the Gregory are not approachable when swells surge against the back side of San Clemente Island. When the waters are flat and calm however, the Gregory offers stunning shallow water wreck diving.

To get onto the wreck site requires a little bit of work, however. The kelp on San Clemente's windward side has experienced a comeback recently, resulting in a bumper crop of macrosystis shrouding the shoreline. Divers will find it necessary to navigate underneath the canopy until reaching the shoreline clearing where the Gregory's wreckage is strewn. Once on the site, bottom time and air supply become minor considerations

A Garibaldi surges back and forth over the encrusted remains of one of the Gregory's engines.

while exploring the 20 to 5-foot depth range of the Gregory. The wreck can still be extremely surgy, even on calm days, but an experienced, relaxed diver will have little trouble negotiating the jumbled and broken wreckage of the shattered destroyer. When the Gregory is divable, visibility is generally quite good, allowing for a complete unobstructed view of the wreck. In the shallows, the blasted hull reveals brass artifacts that glisten like gold as high ambient sunlight sparkles off the bottom. Brass, bronze, and copper pieces of plumbing and machinery are polished to a glossy sheen due to the continual wave action the wreck receives. Huge pipes and twisted iron plates litter the bottom, encrusted with a thin layer of algae. The wreck is mostly broken up, but portions of the engine and deck structures still remain, providing photographers with an excellent resource to fulfill their underwater desires. Those seeking game will find the Gregory to be an excellent producer; pink abalone are waiting underneath the rocky crevices in the neighboring kelp bed, while unusually large calico bass and sheepshead frequent the wreck itself.

Despite deterioration due to its demolition, and the corrosive forces of the sea, there is still a lot left of the Gregory for divers to explore and enjoy.

Artifacts: When divable, the Gregory has been a large producer of marine artifacts. Over the years, many items of brass have been recovered from her. The destroyer has been a frequent yielder of portholes, brass valves, deck fittings, and machinery. There are still many items left on the wreck as swell action and surge precludes her from being dived at times.

Hazards: Planning a dive on the Gregory is always a 50-50 proposition. Swell action along the backside of San Clemente often renders the wreck undivable. Strong surge and waves combined with many sharp pieces of rusting wreckage can be hazardous to a diver's health. Consequently, the site is only divable during mill-pond-like conditions. The back side of San Clemente Island where the Gregory lies can be found most calm during late fall and early winter months.

Divers also need to be especially mindful of the thick kelp bed that encircles the wreck area. Due to the shallowness of the area and exposed rocks near the surface, dive boats generally cannot anchor right next to the wreck. This means divers must swim in to the Gregory by navigating beneath the kelp canopy. Be sure enough air is saved at completion of the dive to swim back to the boat underwater and avoid surface entanglements in the kelp. It should be noted that the kelp bed is extremely pristine and beautiful, making it an added bonus when visiting the Gregory.

Photo Tips: Due to the shallow depths involved when diving the Gregory, tremendous amounts of high ambient light are present on sunny days. The photographer can, when desired, shoot the wreck with available light only. If an extra splash of color is desired when photographing a glistening brass object, a small strobe positioned far from the lens will offer a clear sharp shot with a minimum of backscatter. Even though visibility on the wreck can get quite good, a small amount of surge can still stir up sediment and plant matter from the wreck. Due to these suspended particles in the water, backscatter can present a problem. A photographer maximizing ambient light, without a strobe, can return with an excellent assortment of clean shots.

Almost all of the Gregory's larger structures offer strong photogenic subject possibilities, but on extremely calm days only. When surge is present, the Gregory can slam a photographer and his 15mm lens into a rusting iron spike, or onto the rocky beach: be forewarned. On placid, accessible days however, wide angle photographers can shoot to their hearts' content on the Gregory. They will run out of film long before running out of available bottom time.

And don't neglect the kelp bed that must be invariably traversed while en route to the wreck! Since diving the area near the Gregory is only possible on calm days, the same applies for the nearshore kelp bed. This area is an incredible underwater wilderness with exceptional water clarity, interspersed with white granulated sand and reef, and large concentrations of fish life. Photographers may want to save a few frames for the kelp bed while swimming back to the dive boat.

23. The John C. Butler

Depth to top:	60'	**Built:**	1943
Depth to bottom:	80'	**Sunk:**	1970
Average visibility:	50'	**Cause:**	Naval Target Exercise
Expertise:	Intermediate to expert	**Type:**	Destroyer Escort
Current/surge:	Minimal	**Length/Beam:**	306'/36'
Bottom:	Sand	**Tonnage:**	1,350
Location:	San Clemente Island Northwest Harbor	**Condition:**	Stern section remaining, but deteriorating

History: The John C. Butler was named after a 21-year-old Naval aviation cadet who died in the Battle of Midway in 1942. Ensign Butler was posthumously awarded the Navy Cross after his squadron attacked a Japanese carrier group, sinking 3 ships. His namesake, the DE-339 was laid down by consolidated Steel Corp in Orange, Texas and commissioned March 31, 1944. Under the command of Lt. Commander J. E. Pace, the new destroyer escort began shakedown training off Bermuda and departed for the Pacific on June 5. Sailing through the Panama Canal, she arrived in Pearl Harbor June 26 and engaged in convoy and training operations in July. She departed

Pearl Harbor on August 9 and began screening transports bound for the invasion of the Palavan Islands. After providing anti-aircraft and anti-submarine protection for supporting carriers, she began to prepare for the Leyte Gulf operation scheduled for September.

Assigned to carrier group "Taffy 3," the Butler and her shipmates awoke off the coast of Samar on the morning of October 26 to face a contingent of cruisers and battleships. The Japanese task force, under the command of Admiral Kurita, had slipped into the area during the night and was bearing down on the surprised American flotilla. The 2-hour battle which followed has taken a rightful place among the most memorable actions in naval history. The American carriers launched all planes for an aerial attack. The John C. Butler and her sister ships went to work laying heavy smoke to confuse enemy batteries. A rain squall provided temporary cover for the destroyers to begin their torpedo attacks. The Butler herself turned from the carriers to launch torpedoes, and exchanged gunfire with a heavy cruiser. Admiral C. A. F. Sprague, commander of Taffy 3, described the following development: "At 0925 my mind was occupied with dodging torpedoes when near the bridge I heard one of the signalmen yell '. . . dammit boys, they're getting away!' I could not believe my eyes, but it looked as if the whole Japanese Fleet was retiring."

The Butler went on to participate in the Battles of Iwo Jima and Okinawa. She was later transferred to outer picket duty north of Ie Shima on May 20, 1945 and was attacked by six Kamikaze aircraft. Skillful gunnery downed five of the six planes, one crashing into the Butler. She sustained damage to her mast and antennas only. She was decommissioned June 26, 1946 and joined the reserve fleet in San Diego. She was recommissioned during the Korean Conflict in 1950 and served as a training ship. The John C. Butler received 5 battle stars for World War II service and received the Presidential Unit Citation for her part in the Battle of Samar. She was decommissioned again in 1957 and re-entered the San Diego Reserve Fleet.

The John C. Butler, steaming off Boston Harbor. Courtesy of the National Archives.

Sinking: In 1970, the Butler was towed to San Clemente Island and blown apart for target practice at Northwest Harbor. She sank to the bottom at 80 feet and broke in half. Her bow section was towed out into deeper water and still remains undiscovered. The remaining stern section sits upright in the sand.

The Dive: The Butler has long been a favorite destination among southern California's recreational diver community. She sits in the protected waters of Northwest Harbor, which usually offers calm, clear diving with superb visibility. What remains of the original 306' Butler is a small portion, just about 60 feet of the extreme rear section of her stern. Her rudders are half-buried in the sand. Her aft quarter sits upright with a slight starboard list.

Divers can reach her now-dormant depth charge racks at a shallow depth of 50 feet. The outside of the ship is covered with encrusting algae and pink gorgonian seafans. The stern section rises high above the bottom, sloping downward gradually to the forward quarter where she was blown in half. The cavernous breech where she split reveals an interesting cross section of the ship's two decks; the lower deck is half-buried in the sand. Although starting to peel apart, the upper deck area remains penetrable, and trained divers will enjoy venturing inside.

The first two compartments inside the stern are rather cavernous and can be visited without the use of a light. Venturing farther requires lighting, and lines are an added safety precaution. The starboard compartments are relatively accessible, but dark. The portside compartments require some acrobatics to hurdle over a barricade of debris and conduit to gain access into the rudder compartment. There are several small rooms adjacent to port, some which feature small air pockets (2 to 3 inches high). The rudder compartment interior is home to lobster and rockfish, with the occasional eel hiding inside old pipes and valves. Due to the depth involved, penetrating divers should pay close attention to available air supply. Care should also be taken to preserve inside visibility as careless movements can easily shroud a diver in a flood of rusting silt.

Outside the ship's starboard side rests the remains of a small unidentified barge that is home to a colorful colony of seafans. Divers following a straight line astern of the Butler and the barge for 50 yards will discover the remains of a five-inch gun turret sitting alone in the sand.

Artifacts: Although many artifacts have been removed from the Butler over the years, little remains of recoverable souvenirs today. There are still many large brass pipes and valves inside the ship, but these are generally huge and would require Herculean efforts to remove them, let alone bring them to the surface.

Hazards: As previously mentioned, interior visibility can become easily obliterated if careless fin movement occurs. One way to avoid this is by removing fins prior to venturing inside. This is helpful in negotiating small tight wrecks such as the Butler. When doing this however, make certain that fins are deposited beneath a *heavy* iron plate, or better still, tied to a piece of wreckage. This will ensure that your fins do not float to the surface while you are walking around inside the ship. As in all shipwreck penetration, it is important to ensure that all equipment is streamlined to avoid entanglement on any wires or conduit that hang from ceilings. There are several small air pockets along the ceilings of the wreck. It is not advisable to try to breathe from any of these.

One final note regarding all Northwest Harbor wrecks; the Navy SEAL and UDT teams conduct regular exercises in this area, sometimes even conducting exercises on the wrecks themselves. Northwest Harbor can be closed to private boat traffic with little notice. Consult the weekly "Notice to Mariners" before planning a dive at San Clemente Island.

Photo Tips: There is little invertebrate life on the Butler, making macro photographic subjects a rare commodity. But what the wreck lacks in close-up material it more than makes up in wide angle opportunities. The seafans and depth charge racks on the upper portside deck make excellent photo backdrops. Due to varying light levels and silt, photography inside the wreck itself tends to be a bit more difficult, but good interior shots are well worth the work.

24. The Koka

Depth to top:	15'	**Built:**	1919
Depth to bottom:	20'	**Sunk:**	December 7, 1938
Average visibility:	40'	**Cause:**	Grounding
Expertise:	Novice	**Type:**	Tugboat
Current/surge:	Slight to severe	**Length/Beam:**	156'/30'
Bottom condition:	Terraced reef and rock	**Tonnage:**	1000
Location:	East Point of Northwest Harbor, San Clemente Island	**Condition:**	Scattered in pieces throughout East Point

History: The steel-hulled ocean-going tugboat Koka (AT-31) was originally designated as the Oconee, but renamed Koka when commissioned in February, 1920. Commanded by Lt. (j.g.) J. C. Bauman, she cleared the ways at the Puget Sound Naval yard, and was assigned to the 11th Naval District. After fitting out and passing inspection, she sailed to San Diego Fleet in March. For nearly 18 years she operated out of San Diego along the coast of Southern California performing the various tasks required of a Navy tug. She pulled gunnery and aerial targets, assisted in dockside maintenance work and towed larger ships in and out of the harbor. The tug displaced 1000 tons and carried a crew of 46.

Sinking: Business as usual came to a surprise halt before Christmas in 1937. While cruising off San Clemente Island, the Koka's 14'7'' draft struck the bottom of East Point and ran aground. She was officially decommissioned the same day. Recovery crews went quickly to work removing as much machinery as possible from the stranded vessel. She was later declared unsalvageable and abandoned as a wreck on January 22, 1938. Her name was struck from the Navy list of ships March 2. The ship remained half-submerged on East Point until winter storms pounded her completely beneath the surface.

The Dive: Although her remnants were no longer recognizable from the surface, the Koka still continued to fight destruction while beneath the waves. The force of powerful Pacific swells hammered the tug, pulverizing the vessel into the rocks on the bottom. Little by little, the larger remaining structures were completely demolished. Some became so overgrown with algae that the wreckage was nearly rendered unidentifiable. But the resourceful wreck diver, when aware of what to look for, can rediscover quite a few pieces of the Koka, including brass artifacts hidden by the sea for years.

The water clarity on East Point is usually quite good, allowing divers to comb the scattered wreck site with accuracy. To find her remains, divers must look for algae-covered rocks with unnatural symmetry. Upon closer examination, divers will discover that there is still quite a bit of the Koka strewn about East Point. Sharp edges, straight lines, suspicious-looking deposits of iron, and rust are usually dead give-aways of the former vessel. Divers will encounter iron plates, brass and copper pipe fittings, valves, and various pieces of machinery. Once the eye is trained in what to look for, finding overgrown remnants of the once stalwart tug becomes less difficult. A large kelp bed grows in the area, providing a thick amber canopy draped against the sunlight overhead. Schools of blacksmith, Bass, and territorial Garibaldi inhabit the site, along with the occasional lobster and eel.

Artifacts: Many artifacts have been brought up off the Koka since divers first discovered the tugboat in 1962. Pete Greenwood, former skipper of the dive boat Scuba Queen, salvaged the propeller's 8-foot-tall blades. Serial numbers and the name ''American Ship Building Co.'' were engraved on the blades and helped determine the wreck's identity. Several other divers have recovered brass artifacts such as the ship's Station Watch Bell, valve handles, and flanges.

Hazards: Surge can be quite strong in the shallows on East Point. The area should be avoided during heavy swell periods. Currents can also sweep through the area at times. When the water is calm the Koka is an easy and enjoyable wreck dive to make.

The weekly "Notice to Mariners" should be consulted prior to planning a dive on the Koka. Occasionally the East Point area is closed to boat traffic due to military exercises.

Photo Tips: There are no large photogenic structures left on the Koka. But that doesn't mean you should leave your camera on the dive boat. The kelp bed surrounding the wreck site is home to clear water and masses of fishlife. Since the area is shallow, high levels of ambient light prevail, making the area extremely suitable for available light photographs.

25. The "No Name Tug"

Depth to top:	20'	**Built:**	Unknown
Depth to bottom:	30'	**Sunk:**	Unknown
Average visibility:	40'	**Cause:**	Naval demolition
Expertise:	Novice	**Type:**	Tugboat
Current/surge:	Slight	**Length/Beam:**	65' (length)
Bottom:	Rocky reef	**Tonnage:**	Unknown
Location:	Inside East Point,	**Condition:**	Blown apart
	San Clemente Island, 100 yds from the Koka		

History: Nothing is known at all about the former seagoing days of the small tugboat submerged inside of East Point, San Clemente Island. Since the discovery of the wreck is relatively recent, it is assumed that the small tug was sunk by the U.S. Navy for artillery or underwater demolition practice. The tug has been thoroughly explored by divers hoping to discover a hull number welded across the stern support beams, or a builder's plate, but with no success. As the vessel's name has been extremely difficult to pinpoint, divers and boat captains over the years have come to call the wreck the "No Name."

Sinking: Since the discovery of the No Name, evaluation of the site seemed to determine that the vessel's cause of sinking was the result of gunnery practice by the U.S. Navy. The wheelhouse and all superstructure was removed, indicating that the vessel had been intentionally stripped prior to being used for target practice. A large singular hatch leading below deck where the wheelhouse originally stood allowed divers access to the engine room. The No Name's hull was remarkably intact, save for one large hole ripping into the starboard bow. By the appearance of the damage it seems as though the tug took a direct hit at the waterline. The steel decks were relatively clean and railings had little growth on them. From 1984 to 1986 the tug sat upright in a rocky boulder-strewn area within a thick kelp bed, not far from shore.

In 1986 the No Name underwent a second underwater demolition exercise. This time the formerly intact tug was blown apart by a powerful explosion. Today, the tug is now upside down, with much of its machinery scattered across a wide area. Engine blocks weighing 500 lbs were lifted and relocated more than 50 yards from the shattered hull. Large valves, heavy pipe, iron plates, and other marine hardware items are littered throughout the site.

The Dive: Like the Koka, the No Name wreck is situated in a picturesque kelp bed. The area is shallow, surrounded by boulders and rocks. The kelp growth is generally thick, causing divers to rely heavily on underwater navigation to access the wreck, and sometimes making it difficult for dive boats to locate.

Prior to its secondary explosion, the No Name was considered one of California's easiest penetration dives. The after compartment could be easily accessed by swimming down through the engine room hatchway. This was a large area filled with machinery, pipes, valves, and what appeared to be large storage tanks. The forward bulkhead was also penetrable by squeezing through the hole blown into the starboard bow section. Here, divers wedged themselves inside by squeezing between the rocks on the bottom and the iron tear. Once inside, they saw a large compartment full of brass pipes, valves, switchpanels, and pumps. This area was much like walking into a brass hunter's supermarket. All items were securely fastened, requiring a tremendous amount of effort to remove them. This all changed forever in the winter of 1986.

Blown apart by the force of a powerful, secondary explosion, the No Name now sits upside down in the same picturesque clearing, although rearranged slightly. The areas where divers once gained penetration access: the engine room and forward bulkhead, no longer exist. Once on the site, divers will quickly discover that the small tug left an extensive legacy: all of the brass treasures inside the forward quarter were jangled loose like a child shaking pennies out of a piggy bank.

Amidst the marine relics, lies what is now left of the former tug boat. No longer penetrable, the entire tug is upside down. The bow and stern section still provide reminders of its former identity, but very few other remnants are as recognizable. The midships section of the No Name sits shattered, its back not completely broken. The wreckage occupies a slightly larger area than it did originally, as the secondary explosion appeared to be significantly more powerful than the original.

Artifacts: After the second explosion, inspection of the scattered debris revealed a treasure trove of brass artifacts. These pieces come in all sizes and shapes. Valves, flanges, levers, and pipe fittings were tossed across the bottom. Many of these items were quickly recovered by sport divers when

Diver Kathy Hill examines some of the brass machinery blown from the No Name tug during its secondary demolition.

The shattered deck of the No Name tug is fringed with kelp and other marine flora.

reports of the explosion circulated. Today, the brass pickings are not as abundant as in the past, but "treasure" still remains for those willing to scour the rocks to find it. Larger pieces, such as the 500 pound engine block, still remain. The question most brass hounds would ask themselves once the item is floating on the surface is "How do I get that thing on the boat?".

Hazards: Like the nearby Koka, the No Name is an easy and enjoyable dive. Surge is very minimal due to the wreck's close proximity to the calm waters of Northwest Harbor. Current rarely prevails in this area.

As with all other sites within the Northwest Harbor area, the weekly "Notice to Mariners" report should be consulted before planning a dive on the No Name. Occasionally this portion of the island is closed to all civilian watercraft due to military exercises in progress (which can mean blowing up ships!).

Photo Tips: There are a few large, dramatic structures that provide interesting photographic subject material. These are all generally found near the bow and midships portion of the vessel. The inverted forward half of the tug provides some interesting angles. Be sure to put a diver in the foreground of the shot to give it some size determination; the bow is still relatively large.

The surrounding kelp bed, with its occasional interspersion of wreckage, is an extremely suitable area for wide-angle and marinelife photography. Here, like the Gregory, large calico bass dart in and out of clearings. While not the most cooperative fish to photograph, these big bass tend to be more tolerant of cameras than spearguns, and can occasionally be talked into posing briefly.

5

San Diego County

26. The N.O.S.C. Tower

Depth to top:	30'	**Built:**	1959
Depth to bottom:	60'	**Sunk:**	1988
Average visibility:	20'	**Cause:**	Storm
Expertise:	Novice to Intermediate	**Type:**	Research Tower
Current/surge:	Slight to severe	**Length/Beam:**	Support structure 70' tall with Lab quarters 30' tall
Bottom:	Sand	**Tonnage:**	Undetermined
Location:	1 mile off Mission Beach	**Condition:**	Twisted and broken up

History: While the N.O.S.C. (Naval Ocean Systems Center) Tower is not a shipwreck in the true sense of the word, it is a wreck bigger and more extensive than many vessels found submerged off the California coast. For those reasons and more, the N.O.S.C. Tower has rightfully found its niche in the west coast submerged-resource scheme of things.

When one thinks of towers, one usually thinks of oil rigs or structures similar to the well known "Texas Tower" (a military early warning station built on the east coast during WWII). On a smaller scale, San Diego's N.O.S.C Tower has striking similarities to both. The Tower was a common sight along the Mission Beach waterfront for many years. It was built by the U.S. Navy in 1951 to conduct oceanographical tests in conditions that represented those encountered in open sea. The site chosen was ideal for such testing; right in the middle of an open stretch of water off the Mission Beach coast, completely open to swells. This created an ideal oceanic environment for research. Twenty-seven years later however, this proved to be more than the structure could handle.

The Tower was never a stranger to the San Diego diving scene. Sport divers have long been visiting the site. It was a structure that offered diving similar to that found on oil rigs. Rig diving is extremely limited in California; although there are many rigs situated off the west coast, strong legal restrictions inhibit public access. The N.O.S.C. Tower provided divers with "rig style" experiences a short distance from shore. The researchers working on the Tower during the week conducted seawater analyses and current experiments. The oceanographers also made in-water observations using scuba equipment. The Tower also at one time featured a vertical rail system that carried a large cylindrical dome into the water. This acrylic 1 atmospheric "ball" could carry two observers down the rail and into the sea to the Tower's base. Here researchers would spend prolonged periods of time studying the marine environment and "ride the rail" back to their live-aboard work station. The ball was removed several years ago and is currently stored on the Naval base at San Diego.

Prior to its sinking, the Tower had been leased to the nearby Scripps Institute of Oceanography, which continued to use the facility as a research station.

Sinking: The powerful winter storm in January, 1988, hosted 15 to 20-foot swells that hammered the local waterfront, causing serious damage. The storm was so severe that piers crashed into the sea from Laguna Beach to Santa Monica. Giant surf flooded coastal homes, destroyed marina property and damaged oceanside inns and restaurants. Engineers who designed the Tower never expected it to have a life expectancy of more than 12 years, and it surprised many by lasting as long as it did. In years past, the Tower had remarkably survived poundings from waves of 12 feet. But the stalwart Tower proved no match for the surf and gale force winds of "Big Monday." Sometime on January 18 the Tower crashed beneath the wild and windswept surface. After the storm moved on, San Diego residents were surprised to find the long-familiar Tower had vanished from sight.

The Dive: The Tower has always been a tremendous diving resource. Local San Diego divers have visited the Tower for years as it offered

Al Bruton explores the wreckage of the NOSC Tower. Photograph by Tom Phillipp.

phenomenal diving opportunities for both the underwater hunter and photographer. Due to its oceanic conditions, pelagic fish such as yellowtail and bonita would visit the area, giving spearfishermen the opportunity to try to land a "big one." At the same time, the beams that supported the Tower had become home to thousands of brightly colored club-tipped anemones, starfish, barnacles, and scallops. The area has long been a fishermens' hotspot as massive schools of perch, bass, and reef fish swarmed the site continually.

Today much of the Tower remains the same, while much of it is remarkably different. The beams and supports once adorned with vibrant invertebrate life are broken. As the Tower twisted at its base and crashed to the bottom, the invertebrate colonies were relocated. Many of these filter-feeders were denied their previously abundant food source after being removed from the current's direct path. Invertebrate life is expected to reforest and repopulate the Tower in time. The good news is that schools of fish still teem through the columns and pillars. Today the formerly above-water portions of the Tower now rest beneath the surface among the twisted and broken supports and beams, providing a significantly more extensive resource than the former structure. The giant waves that smashed against the Tower on "Big Monday" apparently caused major structural damage before sending it to the bottom. The path of wreckage indicates that the four-legged structure snapped at two base supports and spun 180 degrees before crashing into the sea. The Tower wreckage site can be likened to a small unfinished skyscraper; divers can easily swim over the remaining girder works and beams, twisted cable, and the shattered enclosures that once housed the research station. The massive pillars lie along the sand bottom where divers can pick and choose their depth from 30 to 60 feet.

Artifacts: It appears that the Tower will receive the same artificial reef status currently afforded to the El Rey, whereby nothing may lawfully be removed from her. The beautiful brass ship's cage lamps that once were mounted on its outside decks however, were apparently removed by brave and enterprising salvors immediately after (or during the tail end of) the storm.

Hazards: Diving the Tower can at times, prove to be hazardous. Given its open-ocean position, the Tower has long been noted for strong surge. Combined with its newer element of jagged metal, snapped steel, and coils of heavy cable strewn throughout the site, a potential recipe for disaster is present unless proper precautions are taken. Because of this it is advisable to not dive the Tower during periods of large swell and subsequent surge. This will help divers avoid the unpleasantries of being skewered on spear-like projections that rest on the bottom. Divers should also take care not to enter tight areas of collapsed wreckage, as much cable and debris still litters the area, making entanglement a distinct possibility for the untrained.

Photo Tips: The wreckage of the Tower offers photographers a wide variety of choices. When the water is clear the abundance of fish life and variety of structures gives the wide-angle photographer much material to work with. The macro photographer will discover that a substantial representation of invertebrate life still remains, although not in the profusion that covered the supports when the Tower was standing.

27. The El Rey

Depth to top:	50'	**Built:**	1946
Depth to bottom:	90'	**Sunk:**	1987
Average visibility:	20'	**Cause:**	Demolition for reef program
Expertise:	Intermediate to Advanced	**Type:**	Kelp harvester
Current/Surge:	Slight	**Length/Beam:**	100'/32'
Bottom:	Sand	**Tonnage:**	133 tons
Location:	1.5 miles in front the Mission Bay breakwater. Large Dept. of Fish and Game buoy marks site.	**Condition:**	Relatively intact.

History: The word "El Rey" is Spanish for "the king." As one of San Diego's newest and largest shipwrecks, the El Rey certainly takes those honors. The Kelp harvester El Rey was previously owned by the Kelco Company and used extensively in the mariculture field. Its job was to gather kelp from as far south as Mexico to as far north as Point Conception. The

The kelp harvester El Rey off San Diego. Courtesy of the Kelco Company.

El Rey was one of Kelco's earlier harvesters, although not the earliest. She was built at Gunderson Brothers shipyard in Portland, Oregon. At the time of her launching she was fitted with four GMC 671 engines. Each engine powered a single propeller. The GMCs were later replaced with two 553 Caterpillars, providing greater efficiency.

The El Rey had the capacity to harvest 300 tons of Macrosystis Pyrifera per voyage. The vessel accomplished this heavy task by carrying water in six special ballast tanks that provided added stability. The huge kelp harvesting mechanism located on the bow would drag the plants on board while a small bulldozer pushed the load toward the wheelhouse on the aft quarter of the ship. As the kelp was piled higher onboard, the seawater ballast would be discharged. "The King" was a busy vessel during its reign. Through the course of its 35-year kelp harvesting history, the El Rey completed approximately 3,600 voyages, traveling more than 810,000 miles in its lifetime. After many years of service, the aging El Rey was decommissioned in 1981 and awaited its fate in the scrapyard.

During its lifetime on the high seas, the vessel did more than just farm the marine environment. Many times during her voyages, oceanographic researchers from Scripps Institute hitched rides seaward to study various sea creatures, including migrating whales. Because of the ship's close relationship with the environment, officials of the Kelco Company were happy to see that the El Rey's final fate was more worthwhile than being reduced to marine scrap: through the efforts of the San Diego Diving Instructors Association and other agencies, she was slated to become part of the Mission Beach artificial reef program.

Sinking: When the San Diego Council of Diving Instructors, along with the California Department of Fish and Game began to plan an artificial reef program that called for the sinking of several ships, one of the trickier logistical problems was finding a vessel suitable for the task. The purpose of the program was twofold: To provide new reefs off the sandy flats of Mission Beach, and to benefit the local recreational diver community with new underwater resources. As timing had it, the El Rey was donated by the Kelco Company for the project. The vessel was thoroughly stripped and prepped for its date with the bottom. Fuel lines and engines were removed. Machinery was taken out of the below decks areas. To make the entire ship diver-safe, several large holes were cut in the deck to allow easy entry and egress for divers. The engine room was steam cleaned to avoid any possibility of contaminating the environment. In the spring of 1987, the El Rey was towed to the Mission Beach area where U.S. Navy Underwater Demolition Team Specialists utilized the El Rey for Naval exercises. Limpet mines were placed on her hull and detonated, and the El Rey went quietly and quickly to the bottom as an artificial reef.

The Dive: Divers visiting the El Rey shortly after she was put down reported a wreck that was still not completely stable. Weather had been less than cooperative. Surge was high and visibility was only marginal. Much of the El Rey uttered a woeful lament as metal and wood buckled and pitched in the surge. Loose pipes and railings flew about, making her less than user-friendly. Wooden framework groaned and creaked with alarming severity. It was soon discovered that the surge had removed the base of a large wall from its foundation and was rocking it back and forth several feet in each direction.

A short time later, the El Rey settled down and was completely classified as "diver safe" by the shipwreck committee members of the San Diego Dive Instructors Association. Today, visiting divers will discover that the El Rey offers much in the way of wreck diving adventure. On exceptionally clear days the wreck can be visible from the surface, with schools of blacksmith teeming over the massive kelp harvesting mechanism. The jaws of the harvester dig into the sand bottom while the hinged cantilever rests pointing skyward. The main deck area is a flat and open iron surface. It is easy to imagine a small bulldozer scurrying about the deck, shoving heaps of kelp up against the tall iron bulwark to the stern. Large holes have been cut into the deck allowing divers to penetrate the engine room and ballast tanks. Here, overhead access is restricted, but there are enough holes to access sufficient ambient light, allowing divers to keep exit areas in full view at all times. On surgy days these openings can force a lot of water through, resulting in a torrential tidal flow. When these conditions prevail it is a good idea to stay out of the ship's interior.

On the main deck, the once-towering wheelhouse is no longer intact, but its girders and beams still remain. This area probably offers the best photographic opportunities on the wreck. There are still ladders, railings, stairs, and pipe vents where the wheelhouse used to be. The plywood walls

The El Rey's stern superstructure is a haven for schools of small fish.

along the main deck have caved in during winter storms. One intact hallway remains along with the head. The remainder of the walls fell on top of themselves like a house of cards. Along the stern, the letters El Rey to port and San Diego to starboard are still legible. The rudders dig deep into the sand.

Artifacts: Since the ship enjoys artificial reef status, local divers have agreed not to salvage any remaining parts of the ship. The majority of brass and items of value were removed before her sinking. The treasure that the El Rey offers today is a highly photogenic structure that is a new home to throngs of marine life. Its layout and intact hull afford adventure for a variety of wreck divers with differing degrees of experience.

Hazards: Since Mission Beach is open to large ocean swells at times, the El Rey can experience very strong surge. When these conditions exist divers should take care to stay clear of hatchways and iron railings so they do not get hurled headlong into them. Boat traffic can also be quite heavy, especially on weekends during the summer months. Because of this divers should descend and ascend along the chain anchoring the Fish and Game buoy to the wreck site. If you bring a small boat to the wreck, you may find other divers anchored on the site as well. It is recommended to tie onto the buoy, or raft onto a nearby boat. This helps avoid falling anchors dropping on top of divers while they are underwater.

Photo Tips: As the El Rey is a young wreck, invertebrate life has just begun to appear. This is only temporary as the process of marine encrustation is an ongoing one. Due to the fact that the El Rey sits alone in a vast desert of sand, fish are heavily drawn to it already, making the wreck an excellent area for fish photography. It is certain that an abundance of invertebrate subject material will appear as the wreck continues to lie on the bottom.

The massive kelp harvesting mechanism on the bow and wheelhouse girders and beams to the stern make excellent structural photographic opportunities for wide-angle cameramen. Since the wreck is so intact the entire vessel offers photographic possibilities that are limited only by the diver's imagination, skill, and equipment.

28. The Shooter's Fantasy

Depth to top:	65'	**Built:**	1955
Depth to bottom:	75'	**Sunk:**	1986
Average visibility:	20'	**Cause:**	Explosion
Expertise:	Intermediate to Advanced	**Type:**	Sportfisher
Current/Surge:	Slight to severe	**Length/Beam:**	65' (length)

| **Bottom:** | Sand | **Tonnage:** | 80 tons |
| **Location:** | In front of Mission Bay Breakwater. | **Condition:** | Wheelhouse and above deck cabin completely removed. Hull and interior intact. |

History: The wreck Shooter's Fantasy has always been, and perhaps will always be to a degree, a mystery ship. Her arrival in San Diego and her subsequent sinking will probably always be a bit vague, but mysteries are always part of shipwrecks and sea stories.

According to San Diego authorities, the vessel Betty Lou floated down the California coast in 1985. Aboard was Dominic Salenti (a.k.a. "Shooter"), his wife, three children, and six other adults. The vessel had drifted without power for several days due to engine failure. Later, it ran aground at Imperial Beach. Faced with the prospect of watching the steel hulled sportfisher crash into the municipal pier, the Imperial Beach City council voted to have the Betty Lou towed to the San Diego Bay Embarcadero. Meanwhile, Salenti reported that he had purchased the ship from its owner in Long Beach. Once the vessel arrived in San Diego Bay, he repainted it and renamed it Shooter's Fantasy. Unable to travel under her own power, the Shooter's Fantasy remained at anchor near the Grape Street pier. According to local officials, during this period many items in the vicinity of the boat began to disappear. Reports of lost bicycles, outboard engines, tools, and marine hardware began to circulate around the waterfront. Coincidentally, these claims began shortly after "Shooter" and his Fantasy arrived. Meanwhile, it was never known for certain if "Shooter" repaired his vessel to operate under its own power. The 80-ton sportfisher didn't budge. It just sat near the Grape Street Pier while "Shooter" and his entourage continued to live aboard the boat.

Sinking: According to Harbor Police, early one morning in October of 1986 an explosion rocked the vessel. The ship went quickly to the bottom. No one was injured in the incident. Salenti was later ordered to raise the ship and remove the derelict as it was a hazard to harbor navigation.

Salenti then began attempts to surface the Shooters Fantasy by himself. He began by "borrowing" neglected boats that formerly sat around the Grape Street Pier and tying them onto the sunken vessel in hopes of raising it somehow. According to local fishermen, all Salenti succeeded in doing was sinking the smaller boats right next to the larger one, creating a bigger mess along the waterfront. After 100 days, the port district granted "Shooter" an extension to raise his vessel. The extension expired. "Shooter" disappeared. The hulk later became property for the port district to dispose of. The former sportfisher subsequently became part of the Mission Beach artificial reef project.

The stairway leading into the Shooters Fantasy.

In 1987 the Shooter's Fantasy found her final resting place. A crew of divers attached giant lift bags to the vessel and raised her off the bottom. Slowly, the rails of the hulk rose to the surface and the vessel was towed on its last ride seaward. Once over the reef site, the lift bags were deflated and the Shooters Fantasy sailed silently to the bottom.

The Dive: The Shooter's Fantasy sits upright on the sand bottom. Her above decks are stripped clean, all is gone except her railings and a mast and boom. She lists slightly, and since she is not a very heavy ship, she does get moved around a little when large swells create strong surge on the bottom. Although small, the Shooter's Fantasy still packs ample wreck diving excitement.

And true to form for shipwrecks, the environment is one of constant change. The huge storm of January 1988 actually picked the wreck up and moved it several hundred yards away from the neighboring El Rey. Prior to this, divers could almost swim from one wreck to another, and the locations were easily identifiable by the large Fish and Game buoys attached to the wrecks themselves. During the storm (one of the largest in recent history with waves cresting upwards of 20 feet), the buoy marking the Shooter's Fantasy became detached. The vessel was relocated shortly afterward.

The above deck area of the Shooter's Fantasy is stripped relatively bare save for its railings and mast. A large hole where the wheelhouse used to be reveals the opening to the stairway. Astern, a small opening still contains the boat's engines. For the experienced, the Shooter's interior is easily penetrable. Although lights are highly recommended inside, there is adequate daylight penetrating most of the compartments. But this does not mean that swimming inside the cabin is for any novice either; there remain substantial amounts of debris in the various rooms. Silt can be stirred up very easily. It is recommended that divers remove their fins and tie them to the railing before going in. The first thing divers will notice is the galley. The sink and furnishings are still intact. Prior to the storm, several large mixing bowls sat upon the counter. There are several other small rooms that divers can explore, still complete with closets, bunks, mirrors and light furnishings. There is no telling what divers may discover when they look through the debris strewn on the floor. Dresser drawers have revealed everything from cassette tapes to skimpy negligees. The wreck is small and the interior compartments cramped, but it is fun to explore nonetheless.

Marine life has not thronged to this wreck as quickly as other wrecks in the artificial reef program. It is anticipated that as marine encrustation continues the Shooter's Fantasy will become a fitting habitat. For now, its decks and hallways are patrolled by the predatory calico bass, and the occasional halibut visiting the sand flats around the boat.

Artifacts: Because the ship was never brought completely to the surface, a thorough prepping of its interior to make it "diver safe" had not been conducted. The job therefore needed to be completed underwater. A team of volunteer divers was organized to clean the hulk's interior out and make it accessible to the public. This proved to be quite a chore. It was widely recognized that the boat was full of all sorts of waterlogged, reportedly stolen junk, but workers were surprised nonetheless. One stairway leads into the ship's interior; a short distance inside divers discovered the hallways blocked with every kind of junk imaginable. To hasten the endeavor, divers began collecting debris in handfuls, carrying it up the stairs and pitching it over the side. Before long, a curious pile of marine garbage began to heap up along the ship's sides: bicycles, tools, stereos, fishing tackle, batteries, pipes,

The Shooters Fantasy galley with original bowls and utensils still in the sink.

carpet, clothes, record albums, kitchenware, and even large German beer steins. Many of these items have been cleared off the bottom and thrown away, while others have ended up in the salvors' personal possession, namely the German beer steins, several of which were over three feet tall. One of the most difficult aspects of preparing the ship's interior for divers was the large sheets of carpet that had to be removed. When the ship came to the bottom, the carpet pulled up and was floating around inside the wreck like a net. Once removed, access throughout the entire ship was established.

Many small and amusing artifacts were brought up from the wreck during its cleaning-out process. Where the Shooter has not been a goldmine of marine hardware, it has produced quite a junkheap of waterlogged, presumably stolen loot.

Hazards: Although many divers consider the Shooter's Fantasy to be ''no big deal'' in terms of wreck penetration (since there tends to always be a good amount of ambient light filtering in through cracks and holes in the boat), care should still be taken when venturing inside. This is primarily due to the amount of junk still in the boat at the time of this writing. Surge can also be a slight problem. The Shooter's Fantasy finds no protection from large ocean swells and surge can be very strong. Outside the boat, a diver might just get tossed around a little, but inside, the net force of water flowing throughout the compartments can become ferocious. Combine this with loose junk flying around at you underwater and the diver encounters some interesting conditions.

Photo Tips: The Shooter's Fantasy interior allows for some interesting wide-angle work. Its low but constant light level requires that the photographer work with a wide open aperture at 1/60 or 1/30 second in most cases. The stairway and galley probably offer the most interesting structure for photographs. There are also several porthole openings (the ports have been long removed) that offer unique opportunities. As mentioned earlier, there is no high concentration of fish on the wreck at present, save for a few schooling blacksmith that congregate near the mast structure. When the water is clear the mast and railings on the boat make nice subject material as well.

---

29. Ruby E

Depth to top:	55'	**Built:**	1934
Depth to bottom:	85'	**Sunk:**	July 18th, 1989
Average visibility:	15–25'	**Cause:**	For artificial reef project
Expertise:	Novice to advanced	**Type:**	Former Coast Guard Cutter

			converted into commercial fishing vessel
Current/surge:	Mild to strong	**Length/Beam:**	156'/38'
Bottom:	Sand	**Tonnage:**	150 tons
Location:	Off Mission Beach near El Rey in "Wreck Alley"	**Condition:**	Completely intact and penetrable from bow to stern; all decks

History: The Ruby E was originally built in 1934 at the Lake Union & Dry Dock Machine Company in Seattle, Washington, as a U.S. Coast Guard Cutter called the Cayne. She was a classic example of state-of-the-art marine engineering during that period. This long, sleek, powerful vessel featured two massive diesel engines and was originally designed to intercept rum runners during the years of national prohibition.

Unfortunately, the government's procurement department moved a little too slowly in this case because by the time the Cayne was ready to slide off the ways, prohibition had ended and the ship was not needed for its original intent. The Cayne did, however, enter the U.S. Coast Guard Service and performed dutifully for 31 years until she was officially decommissioned in 1965.

She was purchased by private entrepreneurs and converted into the fishing vessel Can Am. Her stern compartments were converted into holds for fish and heavily insulated to keep the catch fresh with ice as she engaged in commerce along the equatorial Pacific. It is reported that the Can Am's cargo was not solely seafood however, as sources indicate she was impounded by customs officials in South America for carrying a cargo of drugs. She was resold in the early 1980's, renamed the Ruby E, and outfitted as a salvage ship. Unfortunately, the new owners found themselves unable to continue their payments on the vessel, and the Ruby E was shortly seized by the bank. She later passed into the possession of the San Diego Tug and Barge Company.

She was heavily salvaged, with her numerous brass portholes and heavy engine room machinery removed and sold for scrap. After the stripping process was complete, the Ruby E was donated to the "Wreck Alley" artificial reef program off Mission Bay in San Diego.

Under the supervision of program coordinator Al Bruton, many private individuals, diving equipment manufacturers, and local dive clubs donated funds to prepare the Ruby E for her date with the bottom. The ship was environmentally cleaned throughout and all possible obstacles to divers were removed. Large holes were cut into the ship in various locations to allow divers easy access. San Diego dive clubs worked together to remove refuse and debris from the old cutter, filling several industrial trash dumpsters in the process.

Sinking: In the early morning hours of July 18th, 1989, the venerable Ruby E was towed to its position offshore from Mission Beach and anchored. Its seacocks were opened and the ship was allowed to fill up with water. The flooding process took longer than organizers expected however, and by noon the vessel had only taken on a slight starboard list. An armada of small craft with eager divers waiting to jump on the vessel, newsmen, television crews, and news helicopters converged on the area.

With a little help from local lifeguards, several large pumps were brought aboard to aid in the flooding process. By 3 p.m. the Ruby E was riding extremely low in the stern. By 3:30, workers had abandoned the ship as she began to sink, rolling slowly onto her starboard side, stern first. With little warning her bow and forward quarter shot dramatically straight into the sky as the Ruby E plunged to the bottom in a geyser of bubbles and foam.

The Dive: Almost miraculously, the Ruby E settled upright, with a slight starboard list, on the sand bottom. At the time of her sinking, the Ruby E's paint was still clearly recognizable with her white wheelhouse and superstructure glowing in the gloomy depths. The Ruby E is an extensive wreck. Divers will find themselves visiting her decks many times to fully appreciate her size.

Since the wreck is buoyed by a large Department of Fish and Game mooring can, she is easily found by divers. Following the line downward will place divers on her bow deck area where they can inspect one of the large penetration holes cut into the chain locker area. Moving toward the bridge, divers will find a large stainless steel plaque bolted and welded into the superstructure. The inscription dedicates the wreck to the diving

The Ruby E's bow section looms vertically, dwarfing the salvage tugboat standing by.

community and the marine environment and lists major contributors who aided placing the Ruby E in the "Wreck Alley" artificial reef project.

From this point divers may enter the Ruby E's wheelhouse (all marine hardwear has been stripped save for the chart cabinet) and officer's quarters. Divers can then access some of the deeper interior compartments, visiting the crew's quarters and inspecting ammunition lockers. A large hole has been burned into the port hull, allowing divers direct access and egress into these rooms in the center of the ship. Divers can then retrace their steps and work their way topside to access the upperdecks again and the engine room hatch.

The engine room is truly immense. Divers can swim down steel catwalks, or through a larger hole burned in the deck to allow easier diver access. The large engine blocks still remain with a variety of brass and steel machinery. Returning to the upper decks, divers can continue to swim astern to the large insulated hold area and a smaller, tighter compartment that housed the Cayne's brig. Dropping over the stern railing a diver will see the name Ruby E clearly. Two huge bronze propellers sit idly a few feet beneath her nameplate.

In all, the Ruby E makes for a fascinating series of dives. San Diego's newest wreck has certainly become a major attraction as divers have already begun a steady migration to her mooring buoy on a daily basis.

Artifacts: The Ruby E is designated as an artificial reef by the California Department of Fish and Game. No artifacts may be removed from her.

Hazards: As a highly penetrable wreck, the Ruby E poses few difficulties for the experienced diver. Shafts of daylight are present in all compartments,

A diver peers inside the Ruby E's bridge and pilothouse.

making her extremely safe to explore. Divers should be aware that surge moving through hatchways can pick up velocity and knock the unwary about at depth. Boat traffic can also be heavy in the area. It is recommended that divers not anchor directly onto the wreck itself (especially if other divers are below at the time), but tie off on the mooring can or raft with other boats and swim down the mooring line.

Photo Tips: As a new wreck, the Ruby E currently has few encrusting marine creatures growing on her, basically precluding macro photography for the time being. However, she offers incredible wide angle opportunities. Her clean superstructure and varying compartments allow wide lens photographers numerous possibilities for setting up shots. Especially good places for a model are the stern (where the ship's name is), the plaque located at the base of the bridge, and the stern mast towering over the Ruby E's decks.

Wreck Diving Safety

Local Emergency Procedures

Santa Barbara/Ventura County

Land Based Protocol: (805) 497-2727 Los Robles Medical Center for Scuba Diving emergencies and transfer to recompression chamber (at Los Robles)

At Sea Protocol: Coast Guard Rescue Coordination Center Marine Radio Distress Channel (16)

Los Angeles/Orange County

Land Based Protocol: (213) 221-4114 L.A. County Medical Alert for Scuba Diving Emergencies and transfer to Recompression Chambers (Cal State Northridge or USC Catalina)

At Sea Protocol: Coast Guard Rescue Coordination Center Marine Radio Distress Channel (16) or phone (213) 590-2225

and/or

Catalina area BAYWATCH Avalon (213) 510-0856

Isthmus (213) 510-0341

San Diego County

Land Based Protocol: 911 or (619) 224-2708 San Diego Lifeguards for Scuba Diving Emergencies and transfer to Recompression Chamber (UCSD)

At Sea Protocol: San Diego Lifeguards or Coast Guard Rescue Coordination Center Marine Radio Distress Channel (16)

Appendix

Local Dive Stores

Santa Barbara/Ventura Counties

The Dive Shop of Santa Maria
1975 B. South Broadway, Santa Maria
(805) 922-0076

Dive West Sports
115 W. Main, Santa Maria
(805) 925-5878

Watersports Unlimited
732 North H. St., Lompoc
(805) 736-1800

Bob's Diving Locker
500 Botello Road, Goleta
(805) 967-4456

Divers Supply of Santa Barbara
5854 Hollister Ave., Goleta
(805) 964-0180

Aquatics of Santa Barbara
5370 Hollister #3, Santa Barbara
(805) 964-8689

Divers Den
22 Anacapa St., Santa Barbara
(805) 963- 8917

Underwater Sports
Breakwater Harbor, Santa Barbara
(805) 962-5400

Aqua Ventures
2172 Pickwick Dr., Camarillo
(805) 647-8344

Aqua Ventures
1001 S. Harbor Blvd., Oxnard
(805) 985-8861

Scuba Luv
704 Thousand Oaks Blvd., Thousand Oaks
(805) 496-1014

Ocean Antics
2359 E. Thompson Blvd., Ventura
(805) 652-1600

Ventura Scuba School
1559 Spinnaker #108, Ventura
(805) 652-0321

Gold Coast Scuba
955 E. Thompson Blvd., Ventura
(805) 652-0321

Poncho's Dive and Tackle
3600 Cabazone Way, Oxnard
(805) 985-4788

Aquatics
695 Channel Islands Blvd., Port Hueneme
(805) 984-DIVE

Far West Marine Center
2941 Willow Lane, Thousand Oaks
(805) 495-3600

Los Angeles County

Sport Chalet Divers
24200 W. Lyons Ave., Valencia
(805) 253-3883

Sport Chalet Divers
920 Foothill Blvd., La Canada
(818) 790-2717

Marina Del Rey Divers
2539 Lincoln Blvd., Marina Del Rey
(213) 827-1131

American Diving
1901 Pacific Coast Highway, Lomita
(213) 326-6663

Dive N' Surf
504 W. Broadway, Redondo Beach
(213) 372-8423

Malibu Divers Inc.
21231 Pacific Coast Highway, Malibu
(213) 456-2396

Scuba Haus
2501 Wilshire Blvd., Santa Monica
(213) 828-2916

Reef Seekers
8642 Wilshire Blvd., Beverly Hills
(213) 652-4990

New England Divers
11830 W. Pico Blvd., West Los Angeles
(213) 477-5021

Sea D' Sea
1911 Catalina Ave., Redondo Beach
(213) 373-6355

Marina Dive & Sport
291 West 22nd Street, San Pedro
(213) 831-5647

Catalina Divers Supply
Pleasure Pier, Avalon, Catalina
(213) 510-0330

Scuba Duba Dive
7126 Reseda Blvd., Reseda
(818) 881-4545

Scuba Luv
22725 Ventura Blvd., Woodland Hills
(818) 346-4799

Pacific Scubanaut
6959 Van Nuys Blvd., Van Nuys
(818) 787-7066

West Coast Divers Supply
16931 Sherman Way, Van Nuys
(818) 708-8136

Divers Edge
18924 Soledad Canyon Rd., Canyon
   Country
(805) 251-DIVE

Desert Scuba
44441 N. Sierra Hwy., Lancaster
(805) 948-8883

Divers Corner
12045 Paramount Blvd., Downey
(213) 869-7702

New England Divers
4148 Viking Way, Long Beach
(213) 421-8939

Scuba Schools of Long Beach
4740 Pacific Coast Highway, Long Beach
(213) 494-4740

Gucciones Scuba Habitat
3220-B S. Brea Canyon Road,
   Diamond Bar
(714) 594-7927

Divers West
2695-#A Foothill Blvd., Pasadena
(818) 796-4287

Southern California Diving Center
1121 S. Glendora Ave., West Covina
(818) 338-8863

Sport Diving West
11501 Whittier Blvd., Whittier
(213) 692-7373

Aqua Adventures Unlimited
2120 West Magnolia, Burbank
(818) 848-2163

Canyon Country Divers
18917 1/2 Soledad Canyon, Canyon
   Country
(805) 252-6955

Orange County

Sport Chalet Divers
16242 Beach Blvd., Huntington Beach
(714) 848-0988

Sport Chalet Divers
27551 Puerta Real, Mission Viejo
(714) 582-3870

Scuba World
1706 Tustin, Orange
(714) 998-6382

Diver's Mart
2036 W. Whittier, La Habra
(213) 594-1311

Scuba Toys
9547 Valley View, Cypress
(714) 527-0430

Black Barts Aquatics
24882 Muirlands, El Toro
(714) 855-2323

Black Barts Aquatics
34145 Pacific Coast Highway, Dana Point
(714) 496-5891

Mr. Scuba
1031 S. Pacific Coast Highway, Laguna
  Beach
(714) 494-4146

Mr. Scuba
13544 Newport Ave., Tustin
(714) 838-6483

The Dive Shop
16475 Harbor Blvd., Fountain Valley
(714) 531-5838

National Scuba
16442-A Gothard St., Huntington Beach
(714) 847-4386

Aquatic Center
4535 Pacific Coast Highway, Newport
  Beach
(714) 650-5440

Laguna Sea Sports
2146 Newport Blvd., Costa Mesa
(714) 645-5820

Laguna Sea Sports
925 N. Pacific Coast Highway, Laguna
  Beach
(714) 494-6965

Adventures In Diving
31678 Pacific Coast highway, South
  Laguna Beach
(714) 499-4517

Ocean Rhythms
27601-#19 Forbes Rd., Laguna Miguel
(714) 582-3883

Sea Ventures
143 North Raymond, Fullerton
(714) 447-3483

San Diego County

Sport Chalet Divers
Vineyard Shopping Center, Escondido
(619) 746-5958

Sport Chalet Divers
5500 Grossmont Center Drive, La Mesa
(619) 463-9381

Sport Chalet Divers
3695 Midway Dr., Point Loma
(619) 224-6777

Sport Chalet Divers
La Jolla Village Dr., La Jolla
(619) 552-0712

Pacific Coast Divers
3809-#108 Plaza Dr., Oceanside
(619) 726-7060

Diving Locker Aquatics
348 East Grand, Escondido
(619) 746-8980

Diving Locker Aquatics
405 N. Highway 101, Solana Beach
(619) 755-6822

Diving Locker Aquatics
1020 Grand Ave., San Diego
(619) 272-1120

W.E.T.
7094 Miramar Road, San Diego
(619) 578-3483

W.E.T.
20 National City Blvd., National City
(619) 477-DIVE

San Diego Divers Supply
7544 La Jolla Blvd., La Jolla
(619) 459-2691

San Diego Divers Supply
4004 Sports Arena Blvd., San Diego
(619) 224-3439

Del Mar Oceansports
1227 Camino Del Mar, Del Mar
(619) 792-1903

Ocean Enterprises
2280 Garnet, San Diego
(619) 581-3483

Ocean Enterprises
267 El Camino Real, Encinitas
(619) 942-3661

Local Charter Boats

Santa Barbara/Ventura Counties

Truth Aquatics
(Vision, Conception, & Truth)
(805) 962-1127

Captain Midnight
(805) 644-7363

Peace
(805) 658-8286

Scuba Luv'r
(805) 496-1014

Excaliber
(805) 529-4080

Sea Ventures
(805) 985-1100

Spectre
(805) 483-6612

Golden Doubloon
(213) 831-5148

Bold Contender
(818) 366-2611

Westerly
(213) 833-6048

Wild Wave
(213) 534-0034

Charisma Charters
(Charisma & Encore)
(213) 326-7460

Maverick
(213) 547-3824

Sea Vue
(213) 548-6129

Mr C
(213) 831-9449

Los Angeles County

CeeRay
(213) 519-0880

Atlantis
(213) 831-6666

Scuba Queen
(213) 691-0423

Argo Diving Services
(213) 510-2208

King Neptune
(213) 510-2616

San Diego County

Horizon
(619) 277-7823

Bottom Scratcher
(619) 224-4997

Sand Dollar
(619) 224-4997

Prince of Tides
(619) 549-4759

Hustler
(619) 222-0391

Local Maritime Museums & Historical Societies

National Maritime Museum
(at the foot of) Polk Street
San Francisco, 94109
(415) 556-9827

Allen Knight Maritime Museum
P.O. Box 805
Calle Principal
Monterey, 93940
(408) 375-2553

Santa Barbara Historical Society
P.O Box 578
136 East Delaguirre
Santa Barbara, 93101
(805)

Santa Barbara Natural History Museum
735 State Street
Santa Barbara, 93101
(805) 966-7107

Ventura Historical Society
100 East Main Street
Ventura, 93001
(805) 653-0323

Santa Monica Historical Society
P.O. Box 3059
Santa Monica, 90403
(213) 828-2170

Los Angeles Maritime Museum
Berth 84, (foot of) 6th St
San Pedro, 90731
(213) 548-7618

Catalina Island Museum
P.O. Box 366
Avalon, 90704
(213) 510-2414

Lompoc Museum
200 South H Street
Lompoc, 93436
(805) 736-3888

Lompoc Historical Society
P.O. Box 88
Lompoc, 93436
(805) 736-6565

The Bancroft Library
University of California at Berkeley
Berkeley, 94720
(415) 642-3781

The California State Library
P.O. Box 942837
Sacramento, 94237-0001
(916) 322-4570

California Historical Society
2090 Jackson Street
San Francisco, 94109
(415) 567-1848

Oakland Museum
Natural Science Dept.
1000 Oak Street
Oakland, 94607
(415) 273-3884

State & Federal Rules and Regulations Regarding Artifact Collection

I. California Public Resources Code, Section 6309: prohibits artifact recovery from a shipwreck submerged within state waters without a salvage permit (3 miles).
II. Channel Islands Marine Sanctuary Regulation: prohibits artifact recovery from a shipwreck submerged within all Park boundary waters within the Channel Island National Park (6 miles).
III. Maritime Law: a Federal ruling that permits artifact recovery on all abandoned shipwrecks within U.S. Federal waters.

*** All divers should be aware that the passage of HR74, the abandoned shipwreck bill, has given individual states the sovereignty to determine and interpet the status of all shipwrecks submerged in state waters. Divers should watch for ongoing developments resulting in increased clarification of this recent legislation.

Author's Note: This book does not intend to encourage artifact recovery, but rather, the preservation of California's shipwrecks for all future divers to enjoy.

Index